DATE DUE			

Sailor of the Air

Sailor of the Air

The 1917–1919 Letters & Diary of
USN CMM/A Irving Edward Sheely

✧

Edited by his nephew
Lawrence D. Sheely

The University of Alabama Press
Tuscaloosa & London

Copyright © 1993

The University of Alabama Press

Tuscaloosa, Alabama 35487–0380

All rights reserved

Manufactured in the United States of America

designed by zig zeigler

The paper on which this book is printed
meets the minimum requirements of American National
Standard for Information Science-Permanence of Paper for
Printed Library Materials, ANSI Z39.48-1984.

Library of Congress Cataloging-in-Publication Data

Sheely, Irving Edward, 1893–1962.

Sailor of the Air : the 1917–1919 letters and diary of USN
CMM/A Irving Edward Sheely / edited by
Lawrence D. Sheely.

p.   cm.

Includes bibliographical references and index.

ISBN 0-8173-0709-5 (alk. paper)

1. Sheely, Irving Edward, 1893–1962—Diaries.   2. Air pilots,
Military—United States—Diaries.   3. World War, 1914–
1918—Aerial operations, American.   4. United States. Navy
Aviation—Diaries.   I. Sheely, Lawrence D.   II. Title.

D606.S48   1993

940.4' 4973' 092—dc20

[B]   93-146

British Library Cataloguing-in-Publication Data available

Now we are names that once were young
And had our will of living weather,
Loved dark pines and the thin moon's feather,
Fought and endured our souls and flung
Our laughter to the ends of earth,
And challenged heaven with our spacious mirth. . . .

And generations unfulfilled,
the heirs of all we struggled for,
Shall here recall the mythic war,
And marvel how we stabbed and killed,
And name us savage, brave, austere,
And none shall think how very young we were.

> *—From "On a Memorial Stone" by Archibald MacLeish,*
> *written in memory of his brother Kenneth MacLeish,*
> *killed in an air battle over Belgium in 1918*

Contents

Acknowledgments

Roger Irving Sheely, son of U.S. Navy Aviation Chief Machinist Mate Irving Edward Sheely, generously offered the 1917–1918 letters, diary, and notebook his father kept while at St. Raphael, France, and over one hundred excellent wartime photographs. Without these artifacts there would be no story. I will be forever grateful to my cousin Roger for permitting me to tell the story of his father's service to our country during World War I and of his place in the early history of U.S. Naval Aviation.

Eva Jane Fisher, niece to Uncle Irving, supplied the all-important April 29, 1918 letter by Uncle Irving. Without it, a lot would have been missed. Aunt Alice Sheely Betts, sister of Irving, supplied much in the way of family history.

R. D. Layman, Jack Perkis, Noel Shirley, Stewart K. Taylor, Lester B. Tucker, Peter F. G. Wright, the late James L. Kerr III, and the members of the Aviation Historical Society of Central New York all provided significant historical data found throughout this text. Friends indeed are these good fellows who generously shared their years of painstaking research.

My son-in-law, Donald Roux, father of a couple of extra fine grandsons, patiently copied many of the old, odd-sized photos that make the words come to life.

My fraternal brother of "The Ancient Craft," Charles Striebig, has been constant throughout in the search to determine the origin and type of Irving's wings. It was the persistance of Bro.

Charles that finally identified them as R.N.A.S. Observer Wings. His is a most generous cabletow.

Geoffrey L. Rossano, author of *The Price of Honor*, the military biography of Lt. Kenneth MacLeish, did more than supply data. He helped and encouraged me when it looked like this work might never be completed. My sincere thanks and my hand in friendship are both offered with gratitude.

For the first twenty years of this effort, my beloved wife, Marion, mother of our treasured daughters, Linda and Susan, was ever constant in her loving encouragement. Together, we hand-copied documents at the National Archives. Then our Lord saw fit to call her from my side.

The manuscript languished.

The Lord blessed me again. Elizabeth came into my life, and again a loving wife saw the worth of this effort. She not only set my mind back to work but also traveled with me to the Archives for more research. In the final months of review and rewrite, my dear "Liz-beth" contributed an editorial professionalism and an agile competence with the computer that brought the countless loose ends together into a coherent document. Without the love and steadfastness of both my daughters and these wonderful wives, this work could never have been completed.

Preface

On October 3, 1962, Franklin and Eva Sheely, my mother and father, received a telegram from Vice Admiral W. R. Smedberg, Chief of Naval Personnel. It stated, "I deeply regret to inform you that your son, Airman Irving Edward Sheely, died Oct. 3, 1962 aboard the aircraft carrier USS Forrestal (CV-59) as a result of a flight deck accident." He was twenty-one years old.

After her initial shock and the grief of the funeral, Mother started to gather and dispose of Irving's pre-Navy possessions.

The hardest thing for her was finding photographs of Irving tucked away in odd, unexpected locations.

A thorough search uncovered more of *brother* Irving's photos and unexpected handfuls of old photos of *Uncle* Irving Edward Sheely when he was in France in 1917–1918.

Two months later, on December 16, 1962, Uncle Irving died suddenly at age sixty-nine.

We created a photo album of brother Irving and prefaced it with these old prints of his namesake, Uncle Irving. Looking at these fifty-year old prints, it was apparent that they represented an untold World War I story of hardship, training from unlikely sources, and moments of combat aviation history. We knew Uncle Irving to be a very private person, but I don't recall any of us ever encouraging him to relate his wartime experiences. Now, he too, was gone.

Once, years before, as he and I sat on his front porch looking across the Albany–Schenectady Road at a military funeral taking place in the new cemetery there, Uncle Irving said softly, "I wonder if anybody remembers?" He said it more to himself than to me.

As that melancholy moment was recalled, I vowed to recover his story from every available source.

It took a lot of very specialized research for which I was totally unschooled. Most of it must be characterized as "muddling through," but with much help and encouragement from real historians and access to his letters and diary, an exciting and very human story emerged, one which I am anxious to share.

It is to both men named IRVING EDWARD SHEELY, who gave so much to our country, that this text is dedicated—

> Eternal Father, strong to save,
> Whose arm hath bound the restless wave,
> Who bidd'st the mighty ocean deep
> Its own appointed limits keep:
> O hear us when we cry to thee
> For those in peril on the sea.
>
> —John B. Dykes, 1861

Sailor of the Air

Introduction

After the German U-boat torpedoed and sank the Cunard liner *Lusitania* on May 7, 1915, with the loss of 1,198 persons including 128 Americans, anti-German sentiment ran high throughout the United States. However, November 1916 saw President Woodrow Wilson reelected to a second term on a neutrality platform. He vigorously pursued his "peace without victory" policy as his solution to the war that raged in Europe since August 1914. In December 1916 it became apparent to both Germany and the Allies that Wilson's conditions for peace were not going to be acceptable to any of the combatants. In January 1917 Germany announced a policy of unrestricted submarine warfare against all shipping either to or from Great Britain. This policy, the president said, violated our rights as a neutral.

The United States broke diplomatic relations with Germany on February 3, 1917.

America's eventual entry into the war was thus assured, and the U.S. Navy was certain to be ordered to deal with the submarine menace in the Atlantic Ocean in general and in and around the European waters in particular. Navy recruiting posters began appearing throughout the big cities.

U.S. Naval Aviation had an inauspicious beginning in 1910, just seven years before. Pensacola became a Naval Air Training Station in 1914 when an aviation unit of nine officers, twenty-three men, and seven aircraft under the command of Lt. J. H. Towers arrived from a primitive aviation camp at Annapolis, Maryland.

Prior to that, on September 24, 1893, in a little house in Newtonville, New York, Irving Edward Sheely became the first-born of Madison and Louisa (nee Forner) Sheely. Irving was followed by Laura in 1895, Madison (later called by his middle name, Lewis) in 1897, Franklin in 1899, and Alice in 1902.

It was not unusual in the early twentieth century for a man to die young, and in 1911, the forty-six-year-old father, Madison, succumbed to illness leaving a widow with her oldest son but seventeen years old. Irving accepted the responsibility and soon became "the man of the house," directing his siblings in all that they should do to help their mother. Mother and family bought a rooming house in Albany to provide some income, and Irving, having just graduated from high school, took a clerk's job with Albany Hardware & Iron Company. He already had an abiding interest and inherent aptitude for things mechanical and used that talent to accept a challenge by an A. H. & I. supplier, Yale & Towne, to pick, promptly, a lock that Y. & T. vowed could not be opened without the key.

Soon after, he moved to a job with the *Albany Times-Union* newspaper. Officials gave him a motorcycle and told him to travel the surrounding countryside and solicit subscriptions for that newspaper. Thus began his love of motorcycling and the eastern New York backcountry. In traveling about on behalf of the *Times-Union*, it was inevitable that the handsome young man of twenty years or so would meet many pretty daughters of farm families. After Irving's four years in the Navy, one of these young women, Dorothy Haskins, became his wife.

A still better paying job and one that challenged his mechanical aptitude lured him into the expanding field of locomotive design as a draftsman with the huge American Locomotive Company in nearby Schenectady. He persuaded both his brothers to join him there, as can be detected in some of Irving's letters.

Then, at twenty-three, with the rest of the world at war and Naval Aviation posters beckoning, Irving knew he would soon have to face a decision about military service. He had faithfully helped his mother through the difficulties of widowhood. By early 1917 she had already remarried, and there were big things stirring in the outside world.

He watched a neighbor, John Callan, later to be Navy Lt. Callan, commander at Moutchic, France, flying over Albany in his Curtiss aeroplane.

He knew he had more to offer than sitting in a muddy trench with a rifle. The Navy aviation recruiting posters challenged him in the new business of flying, and he believed that the Navy would put his mechanical abilities to work with the latest engineering marvels. In March 1917 he enlisted in U.S. Naval Aviation as Landsman (candidate) for Machinist Mate Second Class and left for Pensacola Naval Air Station shortly thereafter.

When he arrived, the Navy did not even have a uniform for him. They rushed him into classes on aircraft engine theory. A week later, on April 6th, Congress declared war on Germany. The strength of aviation within the Navy and Marine Corps combined was: 48 officers and 239 enlisted men, 54 airplanes, 1 airship, and 1 air station.

On orders from Washington, Pensacola base commander Lt. Kenneth Whiting recruited 7 officers and 122 enlisted men as volunteers to become an instant aviation force. Whiting's orders included transporting these untrained, underequipped recruits directly to France to combat the German submarine menace. LMM2c I. E. Sheely was among those enlisted volunteers.

Lt. Whiting was not authorized to take any aircraft with him. Of the fifty-four aircraft on hand, none was combat worthy anyway.

This force became known as the First Aeronautical Detachment and sailed for France on May 25, 1917, aboard two colliers, the USS *Jupiter* and USS *Neptune*. When the *Jupiter* landed its aviation contingent on the west coast of France at Pauillac on the Gironde River on June 5, 1917, and the *Neptune* discharged its Navy men at St. Nazaire on the Loire River on June 8, they became the first organized contingent of American forces to arrive at a World War I zone of combat.

Without the means to train and supply these mostly raw recruits with the weapons of aerial warfare, Lt. Whiting went off to Paris where he was cordially received. The French authorities were only too happy to provide the facilities, the officers, and the aircraft with which to train these men. This cooperation resulted in a portion of his enlisted force being sent to the French Army Aviation training base at Tours for pilot training and the rest to the French Naval Air Training Station at St. Raphael where they were taught aviation mechanics and aerial observation. Irving went to the sunny south shore of France at St. Raphael.

In concert with the men who followed during the next seventeen months, the now splintered First Aeronautical Detachment eventually trained under French, British, and the U.S. Army Air Service. They created their own seaplane training base at Moutchic and huge supply bases at Pauillac and Eastleigh in England. U.S. Naval Aviation was soon flying combat aerial antisubmarine patrol duties at St. Trojan, LeCroisic, Dunkerque, and Killingholme, England. By the end of hostilities, this new branch of the Navy had created twenty-seven aerial patrol bases in England, France, Italy, Ireland, and the Azores.

Had the war lasted another three weeks, they would have

been bombing the German submarine pens in occupied Belgium from their own strategic bombardment force known as the Northern Bombing Group. They had gained access to almost a dozen three-engine Caproni bombers for which they had paid dearly in lives to ferry from Italy north over the Alps.

These men not only had to create a viable military force out of handouts from the French, British, Italians, and a minimal supply from the United States, they had to care for themselves. Irving had to seek out a local dentist at St. Raphael. He found a shoemaker in Dunkerque and the YMCA helped him send money home. While in England, he sought out a place to buy a warm aviation helmet and goggles. At Moutchic, when they needed water, they dug a well. From the start, their cooking was done on open fires. Such a simple creature comfort as a haircut was unavailable, so Irving established himself as the local barber wherever he happened to be, and both he and his buddies appreciated the arrangement. He kept meticulous records, making it possible to identify the men of his outfit.

They were the first to get over there; they gave everything they had and suffered many privations, yet the best General Pershing could find to say about them was that they had an insignificant effect on the outcome of events on the western front.

These recently recruited enlisted men were trained by non-English-speaking French officers and by British officers who tried to make them over into British troops.

Those chosen to become Observer/mechanics learned from this variety of instructors that an Observer did so much more than look over the side of an aircraft and "observe." This man was expected to (1) navigate over water, (2) hit a ground target by dropping aerial bombs, (3) operate an aerial camera, (4) protect his aircraft with a manually swiveled Lewis machine gun,

(5) maintain the French, British, or Italian engine in peak condition so that it would run without stopping throughout a mission, and (6) ensure that all the tension wires that kept the wings and control surfaces attached were trimmed for fail-safe operation.

The pilots were the officers in U.S. Naval Aviation and, for the most part, college boys.

An exception were those enlisted men who completed pilot training at Tours. They too were eventually commissioned because they had to associate with the other officers/aviators. However, enlisted men who were later sent to Britain for combat pilot training with Navy officers were referred to as "Hard Guys" and treated with disdain.

Some of the young officers tried in vain to obtain commissions for their enlisted observers, but Navy leadership took another four years even to recognize the function of the aerial observer. The wings awarded by RNAS/RAF observer schools were disallowed, by directive, as part of the uniform of those who actually flew combat missions as Navy-enlisted observer/gunners. Adm. W. A. Moffett was given the distinction of qualifying as Naval Aviation Observer #1 on June 17, 1922. It was only then that the Navy recognized the rating of Aerial Observer. ("United States Naval Aviation 1910–1970," *Navair* 00-80P-1, [Washington, D.C.: U.S. Government Printing Office, 1970], p. 49)

In France and later in England, enemy shrapnel fell from the sky on Navy Petty Officer (Air) Irving Sheely and burst around him from a sixteen-inch railway gun. It followed him into the sky when he flew, and Irving himself laid it on the enemy thousands of feet below him. For reasons known only to himself, he called it "scrapnel."

The creativity of his mind and the craftsmanship of his hands were the things important to him in a world discovering that it could design, build, and constantly improve machines of complex function—and he was part of it.

The following letters written by Irving plus his diary entries have been combined and set down in chronological order. They are exactly as written by him including spelling and grammar. Only those words that would not be understandable to the reader have been explained. Some cannot be explained. Minor punctuation has been amended only for reading clarity.

Researched data have been added at significant locations to provide insight into the larger events surrounding Irving's activities.

Selected sections of this book were originally published by the League of World War I Aviation Historians in the summer 1988 issue of their journal *Over The Front*.

 CHAPTER I

Enlistment, Pensacola, and Abroad

March 28 to May 24, 1917

From the Service Record of Irving E. Sheely:

Enlisted at Albany, N.Y. March 28, 1917, age 23 as Landsman for Machinist Mate. U.S. Navy serial number: 191-88-09

Wed. March 28, 1917 ✧ *Enlisted in Schenectady—passed the severest exam possible*[1]

Albany Times-Union newspaper article, March 29, 1917:

ALBANY FIRST TO ENLIST NAVAL AVIATION QUOTA — EDWARD E. SHEELY[2] FOURTH TO BE ACCEPTED FOR SERVICE IN CONNECTION WITH AIR SERVICE:

With the enlistment of Edward E. Sheely, 299 Clinton Ave., in the aviation corps of the navy yesterday, the Capital District navy recruiting station, Broadway, in charge of Ensign Philip E. Hambsch, has made a record as being the first recruiting officer to enlist its authorized number. The Albany office was authorized to enlist four.

Mr. Sheely was enlisted as machinist's mate, second class,

---

[1]Enlisted Schenectady, per his diary, sworn in at Albany.
[2]Irving Edward Sheely, not Edward E. Sheely.

and will be sent to the navy aviation station at Pensacola, Fla. He has been connected with the American Locomotive Works at Schenectady and has had much experience with machinery.

Announcement was made that the Albany station has examined a record number of applicants in one month, 175 having been examined . . .

March 29, 1917 ✧ *Busy day getting ready. Said Good-bye to boys at ALCO[3] and Albany Hardware & Iron Co. and did a lot of hustling around*

March 30, 1917 ✧ *Left Albany on 4:45 arrived in New York 7:00 P.M. Stopped over night at Aunt Carrie's[4]*

March 31, 1917 ✧ *Left Penn Station on 9:15 A.M. Settone,[5] Ada and Aunt Laura see me off[6]*

April 1, 1917 ✧ *Engine broke down in So. Carolina but were not delayed long*

April 2, 1917 ✧ *Arrived in Pensacola, Florida 9:45 A.M. Went direct to Aeronautic Station*

[On May 8, 1911, Capt. Washington Irving Chambers, U.S.N., officer in charge of aviation, prepared requisitions for the purchase of two aircraft from the Glenn Curtiss Company of Hammondsport, New York. These first two aircraft were used for pilot training at such diverse

---

[3]American Locomotive Co., Schenectady, N.Y., Irving's employer at time of his enlistment.

[4]Caroline Bowers, paternal aunt.

[5]Settone Bowers, Irving's cousin and son of Aunt Carrie.

[6]Laura Kilmer, paternal aunt, and her daughter Ada.

U.S. Navy L.M.M.2c Irving E. Sheely, age twenty-three, about to leave from his home at 299 Clinton Avenue, Albany, New York, on March 30, 1917, for Pensacola NAS (Courtesy of Roger Sheely)

locations as Annapolis, Maryland, Hammondsport, New York, and San Diego, California. A permanent station for naval aviation was not available until the old Navy Yard at Pensacola, Florida, was put back into operation in January 1914. It became the first Navy base dedicated solely to aviation training and experimentation. Pensacola Naval Aeronautic Station has been in constant operation ever since. ("United States Naval Aviation 1910–1970," pp. 4–9)]

U.S. Aeronautic Station
Pensacola, Florida
April 5, 1917

Dear Everybody,–

How's that for writing to the whole bunch at once? It's pretty hot down here so I won't be able to write to each one separately. Besides we have lots to do. Get up at 7:00 A.M. breakfast at 7:30 and mustered in at 8:00. Mustered in is the same as roll call. We have a large dining room or mess hall they call it here and they have pretty good feeds. The only objection I have is they don't give you milk in your tea or coffee. I guess I'll have to get use to it though. Thats one of their by rules or mottos "What you don't like you'll have to get use to". From 8:00 till 9:00 we have military drilling and at present the rest of the day is to ourselves. But starting Monday we will have to go to class. There are different buildings just the same as at Union College.[7] For instance there is the copper building the machine building the wood working and then the Flying school. I am not familiar with everything yet, so will leave some to tell later.

---

[7]Union College, Schenectady, N.Y. Irving's brother, Lewis, was a student there at the time.

Pensacola is a pretty little place but we are about four miles from it. The trees and grass are just as green as they can be. Lots of all kinds of birds and sea-gulls.

I have to look sharp some-times to distinguish them from airplanes in the distance. By Gory! but those aeroplanes are flying around all the time as many as fifteen I have counted in the air at once. Some way up. Others only up a little ways. I've been trying to get some pictures of them but they whiz past so dam fast I can't get it on 'em.

It was some long trip down here. When I got to New York, I shook my overcoat. At Washington DC I shook my undercoat. At Savanna, Ga. I shook my vest and when I got here I shook my heavy underwear.

Our uniforms are not ready yet so I am going to ask Lonze, accent on the z, to do a few things for me.[8] First I want my bathing suit. We are right on the beach and the sand is as white as salt. Everybody is in bathing when they are off duty. Next I want my kahki pants. The pair on top, if they are as I left them. If not, the best pair I've got. Not the ones with the laced legs or the ones with the tar on them. Then I want my kahki hat the one with the wide rim. [sketch] Its a soft hat in the store room. Then send me one of my best brown shirts, largest size and also the gray shirt with the soft collar.

I am banging around in my best suit, so the quicker you get these on the way, the sooner I'll like it.

One of the fellows told me that we will have to make drawings and cross-sections of all the different parts of the aeroplane so if you will pick out a few things I need in that line. First I'll need a scale. The one in the leather case in that box I brought down

---

[8]Lonze is a nickname for his youngest brother, Frank.

from ALCO works. A bow pencil, one with the screw adjust-ment in the center, thus [sketch]. A triangle, I don't believe you'll use that small 30–60 so send me that one and the small 45 if you think you can spare it. If you can dig up a large compass for lead, will help out a lot. One of those cheap ones. I think there is one in the top drawer of the wash stand in our room.

One 6H pencil and a 2H or 4H. About 8 of those large head thumb tacks.

Fishing is great down here so send me some fish hooks. In the store room there is a lot of hooks tied on short lines. Lines about a foot long. Send me all of these. There is a box of hooks on the shelf above the wash stand if they are not smaller than illustrated [sketch] send them too.

If you can find some large white line on a wood slat this shape [sketch] send a couple of them.

Wrap all these small things up and put them inside some of the clothes and wrap all together tight and send them by Parcel Post. Ask Mama if she will see that the buttons are on the pants and shirts.

I have tried to explain so you wouldn't have any trouble in finding these things but if you can't, write, and I'll try to explain better.[9]

I am unable to leave these barracks until further notice, or I would send you some money in a registered letter here so I will ask you to please trust me till I can do so. I don't think the P Post will be very much. Be sure to wrap it in as strong paper as you can find and you can use that white fish line to tie it up with. There

---

[9]Frank, Irving's youngest brother, was always considered by Irving to have to be told every detail. However, I always considered my beloved father, Franklin George Sheely, to be the smartest man in the whole world.

is some blank tags in the kitchen cabbinent (I don't know how to spell that darn word anyway) to address them.[10]

Be sure to mark your own address and a (From) in front of it. I am getting all sun-burnt and it hurts like blazes.

I think this will be all for this time hoping this will find you all well, I am

As Ever,
Irving

[*On April 6, 1917, America declared war against the Central Powers comprising the German empire and Austria-Hungary, and, by extension, their allies, Bulgaria and Turkey. This action put America on the side of the Allies and in the end, twelve countries fought against the Central Powers.*]

U.S. Aeronautic Station
Pensacola, Florida
April 15, 1917

Dear Mother,–

Received your letter and also everything forwarded.

Gosh, it takes a long time to get here.

I am getting pretty well settled now. I have my uniform on and I've been to three dances so far in it. We can't get out in civilian clothes but can go anywhere in uniform.

Three of us had our pictures taken and I am sending you one enclosed.

That letter from Canaan was from a girl at one of the farm houses where I stopped. She saw my picture in the paper. I'll bet

---

[10]Irving was a high school graduate, but details like spelling were never important to him.

a great many people have seen it. I mean people where I've stopped last summer.

I sent Glassbrook a card.[11] I can't spend all my time and paper writing everybody.

I received the bundle and also the paper. My! but diden't they throw the bull about the Times Union representative.

I wrote a card to Andy and also Marie Gass.[12]

Did you get my photo back from the Times Union? And did you get my insurance papers.

I am studying all about high speed motors now—started Monday. Hope I can pass those exams.

Tell Lewis I got everything O.K.[13] My little experience in drafting comes in great.

We have to draw cross sections of different parts of motors such as crank shafts, bearings, connecting rods, pistons, cylinders, etc.

We are to get 17.60 per month for the first three months and increase 50% as we qualify.

We have been forwarded about 60.00 worth of clothes. One blue uniform two white uniforms two sets of underwear six pair of socks, one pair of shoes, two hats, one blanket, two sheets, 1 pillow case, two Turkish towels. There are about 200 of us here now from all over the U.S.

Hoping to hear from you soon,
Irving

---

[11]Walter Glassbrook was one of Mother Sheely's roomers.

[12]Andrew Gregg, future brother-in-law. Marie Gass (?).

[13]Madison Lewis Sheely, brother.

Three 1917 recruits from Pensacola NAS, Florida, in their Navy Dress blue uniforms. Left to right: Sheely, Halstead (who would later die in France from an unknown illness), and a third unknown (Courtesy of Roger Sheely)

[*Irving's Service Record shows that on May 1, 1917, while he was at the U.S. Navy Aeronautic Station, Pensacola, his Landsman (candidate) status was dropped, and he was officially rated MM2C (Machinist Mate Second Class).*]

U.S. Aeronautic Station
Pensacola, Florida
May 6, 1917

Dear Laura[14]

Received your letter and I guess its the first one you ever wrote to me. How about it? I've just blotted this and it looks like the big zepplin air ship we have here so I'll leave it. My but its a whooper.[15] I don't pay any attention to aeroplanes any more, they're too common.

Those pictures are very good, but I diden't have a grouch on, the sun was in my eyes instead. I received the paper the other day. I certainly stand in pretty good down there, don't I?

Don't bother sending a paper every day I haven't got time to read it.

Why the du'st don't you answer some of the questions I've asked you such as my insurance papers and picture from the T.U. whether they have come back or not.

I'm surprised to hear about Doom but wish him all the good luck a seafaring man can wish to another.[16]

---

[14]Laura, sister.

[15]The Navy's first airship, the 175-foot DN-1 (Dirigible, Navy, No. 1) was built by the Connecticut Aircraft Co. and received at Pensacola NAS in December 1916. It mounted two 140 hp Sturtevant engines with swiveling propellers, but it was so overweight one engine had to be removed for it to fly. The DN-1 made three flights during April 1917 at Pensacola and was then scrapped. (Gordon Swanborough and Peter Bowers, *United States Navy Aircraft since 1911* [New York: Putnam 1968], p. 481)

[16]Frank Dennis of Hudson, N.Y., with whom Irving worked at Albany Hardware and Iron Co.

But I'm afraid Uncle Sam will have him. You've heard about this Army draft bill being passed. I understand that newly weds are the first to be drafted. I had a letter from Jennie [?] and I answered it today. Also had a letter from Bob[17] Tell him I've had a letter from Olive[18] since I've been here.

I am sorry to hear about Fred Forners[19] wife and hope she is better now.

I wrote a card to Mr. Shrieves.[20] Its a different one than I sent you and the only one I've got. It was given to me.

I am enclosing a money order for ten dollars. I am not going to keep any more money around me than I need. I wish you would give 1.50 to Doom and ask him if he will give it to Sect. Wm. Wensley of Ancient City Lodge #452.[21]

Mr. Wensley sent me by request my certificate which I needed to visit other lodges. This is what he told me it would be ($1.50)

The rest is what I owe Mama and some for express on that package.

If there is enough left I wish you would fix up my pictures that I left with you in a book about 5 x 7 or 5 x 8 and send it to me.

Hoping your are all well, I remain
Irving

---

[17]Robert Mitchell, another resident at mother's rooming house.

[18]Olive Haskins. Irving later married her sister, Dorothy.

[19]Fred Forner, maternal uncle.

[20]Mr. Shrieves, Sunday School teacher.

[21]Albany, N.Y., Lodge of Free and Accepted Masons.

May 8, 1917

Dear Son

I still have no mail from you, but Smith was in the A. H. & I. Co.[22] and some one there said they had a letter from you and so I trust you are well. That is all that pleases me to know that much. If you have much to do and [it is] too hot to write, just drop us a card.

Love,
Mother

[*Irving's Service Record shows that on May 10, 1917, his Machinist Mate Second Class Petty Officer rating was amended to include "Air" (MM2C[A]) although he had not yet been up in an airplane. However, he had enlisted as an aviation candidate.*]

[Postcard]

U.S. Aeronautic Station
Pensacola, Florida
Apr. 9, 1917[23]

Dear Mother:

Am sending my civilian clothes home also my camera and my cuff buttons in pocket.

Don't need them down here any more.

---

[22]Cyrus Smith was Irving's stepfather; the Albany Hardware & Iron Co. was Irving's former employer.

[23]Irving made a mistake in the month. Card is postmarked "May."

Received your letter yesterday and will write in a few days, awfully busy.

Don't write till you hear from me again.

I am as ever,

Irving

May 10, 1917 ✧ Volunteered to go with the Aeronautic Detachment.[24]

May 11, 1917 ✧ Busy day gettin ready to leave. Left on the 11:00 P.M.

May 12, 1917 ✧ Passed through Montgomery, Atlanta, Ga. Had dandy weather for traveling

May 13, 1917 ✧ Passed through the Blue Ridge mountains of Virginia

May 14, 1917 ✧ Arrived in Baltimore 1 P.M. went direct to USS Neptune at Sparrows Point.[25]

---

[24]"Following a request from the French ministry of Marine for Naval Aviation personnel, it was decided by the Chief of Naval Operations to send one hundred men to France for training. Lt. K. Whiting, U.S.N. was placed in command and it was decided to send the detachment over on the two colliers, USS Jupiter and USS Neptune. The total force consisted of seven officers and 122 enlisted men." (CDR. Kenneth Whiting, USN, "History of the 1st Aeronautic Detachment, USN," unpublished, Nov. 29, 1918, National Archives, Washington, D.C.)

[25]The balance of the First Aeronautical Detachment boarded the USS *Jupiter* at Hoboken, N.J. Both ships sailed on May 25, 1917. (Log of USS *Jupiter* (AC-3) 1917, and Log of USS *Neptune* (AC-8) 1917, National Archives, Washington D.C.)

Caswell Hotel[26]
Baltimore, Md.
May 14, 1917

Dear Mother,–

I suppose you will be suprised to hear from me up here but I am going somewhere on a ship with 47 others probably to France. None of us are just sure where yet. I am feeling fine had a lovely trip coming north again. We went through Montgomery Ala, Atlanta Georgia, back through Washington D.C. to Baltimore.

Our clothes are on board the ship Neptune and I am writing this while I have a chance down in our locker room. I sent everything I diden't need home. I sent your empty suit case from Baltimore by P.Post. I am suprised [*sic*] you haven't heard from me because I wrote a couple of days before I left Pensacola Fla. and sent an express money order for ten dollars in it. I also wrote a card when I sent the suit case from Fla.

Tell Laura not to bother with the pictures now for I have enough to lug around with out the unnecessary things.

I received your card today from Mr. Simon[27] one from Geo. B. Clapham[28] one from Frank Haskins[29] all forwarded to Baltimore from Pensacola.

---

[26]Writing paper is on Caswell Hotel stationery including a picture of the hotel. Irving drew an arrow to the picture and wrote, "I stayed at this hotel Saturday night."

[27]Lester G. Simon, Minister of Tabernacle (later Temple) Baptist Church, Albany, N.Y.

[28]Deacon at T.B. church.

[29]Father of Olive Haskins.

Frank H. tells me that you have had quite a snow storm and the old Catskill Mts. are covered with about ten inches.

Write and tell me if you have received all these things I've sent you, the suit case with my clothes, the camera, the cuff buttons, the money order and this last suit case.

After I leave, all mail will be censored so I'm afraid I won't be able to tell you as much as I have in this letter.

If they knew what I've told you in this letter I would get another bawling out. I'm getting quite used to them now.

I have to stand watch on the starboard deck every other night from 2 to 4 o'clock in the morning. I don't mind that but its the getting up and the wild way they call you.

Tell Frank that when he wants to know when he is well off to stay the H out of the army and navy.

Thanks that I am in neither but I'm wearing the sailors uniform and I get looked upon as a damn *gob*. Some of the people will get it someday and they will look on the man in the uniform with more respect. I'm not saying that that is the case all the time but it is most of the time.

I understand that we get a new and special uniform soon for aviators. It can't come too quick for I'm sick of being called a GOB when I'm not.

Well, we're all kidding each other about feeding the fishes. You know that is what they say when you get seasick.

I hope there not hungry when I start feeding them.

Its a pretty big boat we're on but hanged if I can say for sure where she is going.[30] In fact I don't care for I'm in for four years and I might as well see all I can while the seeing is good.

---

[30]Only a Navy "Boot" or rookie like Irving would refer to the United States Ship *Neptune* as a "boat."

How is everybody, Mr. Smith,[31] Miss Dorwalt, Miss Brown, Frank Dennis,[32] Alice, Laura, Frank, Lewis and yourself.[33] Hope you are all well and hoping to hear from you soon. I am

As Ever,

Irving

P.S. address

c/o USS Neptune

Baltimore, Md.

May 15, 1917 ❖ *Went ashore and had a dandy time. Rode all day in Hayes Hamman's Pierce Arrow car.*[34]

May 16, 1917 ❖ *Started to stand watch 2 hours on at a time. The transport was being loaded with rails, wheat, flour, and 6 in. rifles. Very disagreeable around the elevators.*

May 17/18, 1917 ❖ *Moved to another wharf only a little way from where we were. Had to rearrange some of the cargo and delayed us a couple of days. (Sunday) Went ashore and had another wonderful time with Haze Hammonds folks. Rode all day in his Pierce Arrow car. Very enjoyable day for the last time on good old American soil for I diden't expect to see it again for a long long time.*

---

[31]Cyrus Smith, Irving's stepfather.

[32]All boarders.

[33]Siblings.

[34]"Hayes Hamman" was later to become Ensign Charles Hazeltine Hammann, Naval Aviator #1494 and winner of the Medal of Honor while flying an Italian-built Macchi flying boat fighter plane. He was killed in the same plane while flying it at a demonstration over Virginia on June 14, 1919.

[*On May 17, 1917, the detachment commander, Lt. Kenneth Whiting, reported on board. The next day Paymaster O. D. Conger, USN,
reported on board. He brought $30,000 (gold coin) for the aviation
detachment.*

*Lt. Godfrey de Courcelles Chevalier also reported on board on May
18, 1917. Chevalier, like Whiting, was a genuine pioneer of U.S.
Naval Aviation. He was a handsome and personable graduate of the
Naval Academy class of 1910. In 1912 he took his flight training at the
Aviation Camp, Annapolis, and was designated Naval Aviator #7. He
commanded at Pensacola and during the war at both Dunkerque NAS,
France, and Eastleigh NAS, England. He made the first landing aboard
the aircraft carrier USS* Langley *(CV-1) on Oct. 26, 1922. On Nov.
14, 1922, he died in the Naval Hospital, Portsmouth, Virginia, from
injuries received in a plane crash two days earlier.*

(Rear Adm. George van Deurs, U.S.N. [Ret.], Wings for the
Fleet, *U.S. Naval Institute, 1966; "United States Naval Aviation,
1910–1970")*]

The Young Men's Christian Association
Baltimore, Md.
May 20, 1917

Dear Alice,–

Received your letter the other day and you said I would owe
you one. So I guess I'll pay up.

I think I'll appoint you my private secretary for the rest don't
answer half the questions I ask. They diden't tell me whether you
received the camera or not or the cuff buttons or whether Frank
Dennis has taken care of that transaction for me or not.

I am sailing tomorrow and today is our last liberty on shore. I
guess we will stop at Norfolk to take on some supplies and then
we are off for France.

I am anxious to see what the place looks like. Tell Lewis I guess I'll have to learn French and anything I can help him out in the French stuff I'll be glad to do it. Ha, Ha.[35]

Well, the next time I write will be from *Gay Pa-rie*. So by – by

Irving

P.S. My address will be
USS Neptune
c/o P.M. New York

May 23, 1917 ❖ *Left Baltimore on the USS Neptune about 5 P.M.*

Norfolk, Va.
May 24, 1917

Dear Frank

Received your letter today and thought I would answer it while I had time.

We are in the Norfolk Navy Yard taking on supplies for our trip across.

We had a dandy sail down Cheseapeake Bay passed through Hampton Roads and saw some of the Atlantic fleet.

Tell Mamma I'm not in the Navy, I'm just getting passage across on this ship.[36] What I've told her is what I've seen. I don't have to do any work, only study, wash my clothes and do a little guard duty.

---

[35]French was required study for brother M. Lewis as an engineering student at Union College, Schenectady, N.Y.

[36]Of course he knows he is in the Navy. He is probably trying to distinguish between being in Naval Aviation as opposed to being a Navy seaman.

And I forgot the eats. I have to do that too, and by the way they are much better on this ship than they were at Pensacola, Fla.

These seamen have to chip rust, paint, and swab decks all day and sleep in a hammock at night. They are allowed a half a pail of fresh water a day to wash with. Wash your clothes then wash you feet then take a bath. Then wash your face and finish with washing your teeth or vice versa all in the same water. How does that appeal to you? Then they say the army is worse than the navy. I'd rather fly than belong to either.

I had a letter from Stoney Creek which you forwarded to me and a card from LeMay.[37] I had a card from Mamma also and tell her not to bother to have my suit pressed and cleaned now for it will be better to wait till I want to use it again and then it will be fresh. Tell her to hang it up in the wardrobe and don't let the moths get in it.

The overcoat you can have if it fits or give it to Lewis if it don't.

I will get a new one when I need one again.

Those shirts and collars you and Lewis can have also the ties.

You see I expect to be away quite a while and when I want to use them again they will be out of style. so you might as well get the use out of them.

I suppose Doom is getting his M.T. trunk [?] in shape. Tell him I wish him and Lucy all the luck and happiness there is.

I wish I had the patience to write to everybody but its all I can do to write home.

Besides every time I start to write I have to give one or two

---

[37]LeMay Sheely, cousin.

envelopes and paper to some of those friends of mine who are always borrowing.

Gosh! but I'd like to take a ride on a motor-cycle again out to the Old Catskill Mts. or up to Lake George.

Those good old trips go flashing through my mind once in a while now, and its pleasant to remember them.

Its a hot afternoon down here in Virginia and I think I'll go up on the poop deck and take a little snooze in the shade and enjoy the gentle Zephers of the Atlantic Ocean.

Hoping to hear from you again soon. I am,

Your brother,
Irving

May 24, 1917 ✧ Stayed overnight in Norfolk at the Navy Y.M.C.A.

CHAPTER 2

USS *Neptune*, France, and St. Raphael

May 25 to August 28, 1917

---

*May 25, 1917 ✧ Left Norfolk about 1:20 Passed Hampton Roads.
Slept for the first time at sea.*

The maritime log of the USS Neptune *for May 25, 1917, states: "(1)
2:18 P.M. cast off from Berth #1 and between 4–6 P.M. were
'Steaming Seaward'. (2) 7:15 P.M. the ship's head was 90 degrees [due
East]. (3) [Because of the ever-present submarine menace they] 'darkened
ship and ran without running lights'. (4) 8:00 P.M. Neptune took
accompanying destroyers USS Perkins (DD-26) and USS Jarvis (DD-
38) in tow but the towing hawser to Jarvis soon parted." [The towing was
presumably being done to conserve coal in the short-range destroyers.]*

---

*May 26, 1917 ✧ Calm and sunny day had a little drilling and
instructions in semaphore.*

May 27, 1917 ✧ Dull and stormy, Ship began to roll a little.

---

*[Towing of the destroyers was still in effect, but the storm tore away the
8-inch line to USS Perkins a little ahead of his bow. The next day, May
28, 1917, the tow line to USS Jarvis also was carried away.]*

May 28, 1917 ✧ *Calm and cloudy. Had instructions in manning life boats.*

May 29, 1917 ✧ *Bright and cheery. Had instructions in International Morse Code.*

May 30, 1917 ✧—*Decoration Day—Had a dandy dinner. Fried chicken, cranberry sauce and everything.*

May 31, 1917 ✧ *Stood watch in the Crows Nest. Several of the fellows were getting seasick.*

June 1, 1917 ✧ *Had rifle practice with the big gun. At sea just a week.*[1]

June 2, 1917 ✧ *Dark and Stormy. ship began to roll terrible. Night found things in an awful state. Rolled out of bed twice. Diden't get any sleep.*

June 3, 1917 ✧ *Sunday—found two life boats smashed to pieces and the waves breaking over the decks still.*

June 4, 1917 ✧ *Started to eat dinner and all the dishes and grub slid into my lap.*

June 5, 1917 ✧ *Had to wear life preservers all the time now and word was passed to sleep with clothes on.*

June 6, 1917 ✧ *Had to stand watches day and night, four on and four off. Was getting somewhat tired of the water.*

June 7, 1917 ✧ *In the war zone. Met the French convoy Wed. afternoon. Wireless warnings that Submarines were following us.*

June 8, 1917 ✧ *Sighted land for the first time in two weeks.*

---

[1]The U.S. Naval Armed Guard Service had recently been formed to provide large gun defense aboard merchant ships, but it is not known if the *Neptune* carried an official Navy gun crew on this crossing.

[*On June 8, 1917, the following was entered into the log of the USS* Neptune:

>   *1:43 A.M. Sighted Pillier Island light.*
>   *Entered mouth of Loire River.*
>   *3:02 A.M. Came to anchor.*
>   *4:05 A.M. Got underway for St. Nazaire.*
>   *6:00 A.M. Secured at dock.*]

June 9, 1917 ✧ *Landed in St. Nazaire. Went ashore and had quite a time. Could not speak to any one. All French.*

June 10, 1917 ✧ *Left St. Nazaire for Brest. Rode all day arrived 10:30 P.M. Slept at Marine Barracks. Went ashore and saw the town.*

June 12, 1917 ✧ *Washed clothes. Went ashore at night, got watch crystal.*

June 13, 1917 ✧ *Left Brest for Camoret only small fishing town.*

June 14, 1917 ✧ *Saw machine the French were flying. Regular flying boats.*

June 15, 1917 ✧ *Machine fell and was completely destroyed. Pilot injured. Mechanic not hurt at all.*

June 16, 1917 ✧ *Submarine warnings coming in every once in a while. From 2 to 6 machines would go out to drop bombs.*

[*LMM(A) George E. Sprague described his experiences with the First Aeronautical Detachment in a 1939 three-part article for* Liberty *magazine entitled "Flying Gobs."*

Having also arrived on the Neptune, *Sprague said they were immediately paid with some of the gold coin brought aboard by paymaster Conger and given liberty for that first day and evening. The next morning they were tumbled out on the dock to spend hours unloading the fifty tons of stores they brought with them and reloading it, in turn, into "40 & 8" boxcars. Rifles were issued, and they immediately entrained for Brest. (Brest is located on the northwest corner of France, one of the principal cities in the Department of Finistere.)*

Upon their arrival, French men and pretty French women "strewed flowers in our path and stuck roses in the muzzles of our rifles as we marched."

They stayed first at a French submarine base. Then they went to a French seaplane station on the coast of Finistere. A barracks was made for them in the town hall of the little fishing village (probably Camaret). There they waited while Lt. Whiting conferred with French authorities in Paris, seeking to secure training facilities for them.]

[Postcard]

June 17, 1917

Mr. Lewis Sheely

Arrived in France OK. Had some trip across. It took just two weeks. I was glad to see land again. We had to watch for submarines all the time four hours on and four off. And my four off the ship rolled so I couldn't get any sleep. This is all censored so I can't tell you very much. I am feeling fine.

Irving

June 17, 1917 ✧ *Dull day. Getting tired of the grub. Takes a cast iron stomach to live on Hard Tack and coffee.*

June 18, 1917 ✧ *Worked on motors. Dissembled the one which fell Friday. 12 American sailors arrived. Their ship had been torpedoed 50 miles from Brest. Were picked up by French patrol boat. Word for transfer again to . . .*

THE AMERICAN ARMY & NAVY Y.M.C.A. OF FRANCE

1st Aeronautic Detachment

June 20, 1917

Dear Lewis,-

Its been quite a while since I received your letter but I have been on the move so much that I haven't had a chance to answer it. Men in the military service don't have to pay any postage so I can begin to save my money, can't I?

I suppose you have been wondering how I got across the big pond. Well, it was some long journey and when I think of the long watch hours and the rough sea, I don't wish the experience over again right away. I looked for submarines so much that I imagined I could see them sometimes. Well, we found out later that there were three after us, but we zig zaged our course so that they missed us.

We were just two weeks on the water. We left Norfolk, Va. on Friday [May 25, 1917] and arrived in St. Nazaire on a Friday [June 8, 1917] two weeks later. It was good to see land again. I shook my sea-legs as quick as I could and started out to see what a city in France looks like.

Well the first thing I found out was that I couldn't talk to anybody nor could I understand a dam word they were saying to me. All I could say was (None Comprehend) and motion my hands, wiggle my head, and I guess they (got me) or understood that I didn't understand them.

I had my money changed and for a twenty dollar gold piece I received a hundred and eight Franc's. That was a hand full but when I bought something, and handed a twenty Franc bill, I got a wagon load for change and then they told me the guy soaked me at that.

This little place where we have been staying is a fishing town but we are going to leave tomorrow for the southern part of

33

France down near Marsailles [*sic*]. I'm getting used to travelling now, and when the word to move is passed around, I don't make as much bones about it as I do the call for mess, simply pack up and be ready.

The French people are very patriotic and a fellow that isn't in uniform is of little or no account, especially in social life.

It's time America wakes up and have some respect for the fellow in uniform rather than look down on him which the majority do.

Its certainly surprising what three years of war will do to a large country like France. There are thousands of Mothers and Widows, dressed in black. There seems to be a pall over all the population. What I mean to say is that there is not much gay life going on, no theater's dances or athletics. At least I haven't seen any yet and I have been in three good size cities and traveled a couple of hundred miles in France too.

Our grub is getting poorer every day. Lots of meals all we get is black coffee and war bread. Sometimes the bread is sour and the coffee is strong enough to poison any ordinary man if he diden't get used to it first.

Well, I suppose I ought to consider myself lucky to be alive and not kicking on the grub.

Yesterday, 13 American sailors were saved when their ship (the Archibold) was torpedoed an sunk only sixty miles off the coast from where we are.[2] They are staying with us till they can go back to America again.

---

[2]The Germans calculated that if they could sink 600,000 tons of allied merchant vessels a month for six months Great Britain would be forced to capitulate. During April 1917 they succeeded in sinking 875,000 tons, but the convoy system, depth charge development, and the advent of aerial patrols finally subdued the U-boat menace. (Theodore Roscoe, *On the Seas and in the Skies* [New York: Hawthorne Books, 1970])

Its interesting to hear them talk about their experience. How they saw the submarine and the periscope and then the terrible explosion and the rush to get in the life boats.

They were in the life boats about five hours when they were picked up by a French patrol boat and brought back to port.

Three of them were killed by the explosion of the torpedo. Some were without hats, some without shirts, some without shoes and such were the way they come in upon us.

We all chipped in and fixed them out with what we could spare and they are feeling pretty happy now.

Aviation is very advanced in France and although there are a lot of accidents and lives lost the Frenchmen are very good fliers.

I also like the type of aeroplane. It is simple of control and very sturdy. They operate their ailerons and rudders [elevator] with one control called a *joy stick* which differs from the American system which is a wheel arrangement.[3]

They have very powerful motors and when they are flying overhead it sounds like the steady even roar of a motorcycle.[4]

I don't think it will be very long before I'll be flying one, and then I'll have some new experiences to tell you about.

---

[3]The Wright system of aircraft control was unique and unnatural to the pilot. Subsequent American aircraft designers adopted the Deperdussion or "Dep" control, which was a wheel that controlled both the elevator and ailerons along with a foot-controlled rudder bar. This was a big improvement over the Wright system, but the much faster joy stick with movements that had good "man-machine relationships" was best suited to the faster and more sensitive combat aircraft that were developed during World War I.

[4]American aircraft engines of the pre-1917 era, such as the Curtiss OX series were struggling to develop 100 hp. The French aircraft engines, with three years of war-demanded performance, were now developing well over 100 hp. Among the most famous European designs were the Le Rhone (120 hp), Clerget (130 hp), Gnome (160 hp), Hispano-Suiza (180 hp), and the Renault (220 hp). [See Appendix B, St. Raphael Class Notebook.]

Well, how are you making out in school? Did you pass all the exams? How does Frank like his new job? Is he getting as much pay as before?

While I think of it in the bottom drawer of the medicine cabinet in our room I left a straight razor. You can have it. I think it is a pipe razor but its a good grade anyway.

Is Mr. Smith having lots of work this summer?

I suppose Frank Dennis is married by this time. I wonder how he likes married life?

I had a letter from Olive while I was at Pensacola but haven't had any since I left Baltimore from anybody.

Well, I guess I've told you all the news so I will close. Hoping you will write as soon as you receive this, I am

Your brother

Irving

June 21, 1917 ✧ *Left Camaret for St. Raphael.[5] Passed through Paris down to Marsailles* [sic].

June 22, 1917 ✧ *Wonderful country. RR passed through a great many tunnels.*

June 23, 1917 ✧ *Arrived St. Raphael. Joined the old fourth Section from Pensacola.*

---

[5]St. Raphael was the French equivalent of the American Pensacola NAS. Lt. Kenneth Whiting, commander of the First Aeronautic Detachment, had now negotiated an agreement with the French to have a portion of his enlisted command trained there by French authority as Observers. This meant training in mechanics, navigation, signaling, bomb dropping, and aerial gunnery. Pilot candidates were sent to a French Army Aviation training field at Tours.

June 24, 1917 ✧ *Went ashore and saw all there was to the town. Tried to talk to some French girls with a Dic.*

June 25, 1917 ✧ *Got up at 4 A.M. and started in with course in aeronautics. Started some barber work.*[6]

June 26, 1917 ✧ *Frenchies were certainly doing some flying. Had some practise in motor erecting.*

June 27, 1917 ✧ *Griffin taught principles of aircraft.*[7] *Also assembled Hispano-Suiza motor in shop.*

June 28, 1917 ✧ *Played football in evening with French.* [Irving probably means soccer.]

June 29, 1917 ✧ *Helped erect a Seaplane and copied down all the details.*[8]

June 30, 1917 ✧ *Did some barber work. Learned timing of Hispano-Suiza motor. Thunder shower in evening.*

July 1, 1917 ✧ *Went to Frejus and St. Raphael and bought a pair of clippers.*[9]

---

[6]This barber work provided his comrades with a much needed service, and he kept their names in his diary while at St. Raphael and later at Moutchic.

[7]Navy Lt. Virgil C. Griffin, born April 18, 1891, in Montgomery, Ala., US Naval Academy, Class of 1912, designated Naval Aviator #41 at Pensacola April 19, 1917. Went overseas with the First Aeronautical Detachment and graduated from the French Aviation School at St. Raphael July 24, 1917, as French Aviator #270. He served Naval Aviation in a multitude of command positions from World War I through World War II and retired from the Navy as Rear Admiral on Jan. 1, 1947, after 38 years of continuous service. He died at the San Diego Naval Hospital, Calif., on March 27, 1957.

[8]Irving created an extensive training notebook that covered (1) assembly and alignment of seaplanes, (2) engine technology, and (3) deflection shooting from the air with a machine gun. (See Appendix B.)

[9]Frejus, small Roman town about a mile west of St. Raphael.

July 2, 1917 ✧ Worked on Salmson motor. Word from Tours that one of the 4th Section boys killed.[10]

July 3, 1917 ✧ One of French Pilots fell and broke his arm. Machine total wreck. this was at St. Raphael station.

July 4, 1917 ✧ Had a half a holiday. Went to Frejus and stayed till 10 o'clock. Saw a perfect eclipse.

July 5, 1917 ✧ Met a girl that could speak English. She had been in the states seven years.

July 6, 1917 ✧ Seaplane fell 200 ft. and pilot seriously injured, prob. will die. Machine total wreck.

July 7, 1917 ✧ Another fell and pilot broke his arm. Wings of plane were wrecked.

July 8, 1917 ✧ Went to St. Raphael and just promenaded the beach. Warm, quiet day.

July 9, 1917 ✧ Started work in the motor shops. Went to moving pictures in evening by invitation from proprietor.

July 10, 1917 ✧ Washed clothes and went swimming in evening.

July 11, 1917 ✧ Did quite a bit of barber work.

July 12, 1917 ✧ Machine fell and Pilot was instantly killed. Our fellows helped dig him out of the wreckage

July 13, 1917 ✧ Went on the beach for three days of instructions.

July 14, 1917 ✧ French holiday [Bastille Day] Went to Cannes. Had

---

[10]June 28, 1917. Thomas W. Barrett, the first Navy airman killed in France in World War I. (Adrian O. Van Wyen, "Naval Aviation in WWI," *Naval Aviation News* [Washington, D.C.: Chief of Naval Operations, U.S. Government Printing Office, 1969], p. 9)

*wonderful time with some Canadian Nurses. Motored to Nice. Mail
from States.*

July 15, 1917 ✧ *Went to Cannes again and by inv. had another splendid
time. Were joyously received by French at Hospital.*

July 16, 1917 ✧ *Payday. drawed [sic] 281 Francs. Went in swimming
in the evening.*

July 17, 1917 ✧ *Wrote to Miss Johnston. Went swimming just learning
to dive.*

July 18, 1917 ✧ *Washed my blues and went swimming. Worked in
erecting shop all day erecting a seaplane.*

July 19, 1917 ✧ *Swimming again. Halstead began to act queer. Finally
loses his mind entirely.*[11]

July 20, 1917 ✧ *Grub continues to be rotten.*

July 21, 1917 ✧ *Letter from Haze Hammond [Hammann]. He stated
that the fellows at Tours were having a few accidents and smashed up
a few of the machine[s].*

July 22, 1917 ✧ *Went to Cannes and had some swimming party.
Nurses sure give us a good time.*

July 23, 1917 ✧ *Started the Observers course, bomb dropping, machine
gun practise, semaphore, wireless operating International Morse
Code.*

---

[11]The name Halstead does not appear on the May 1917 boarding manifest
of either *Jupiter* or *Neptune*, but in Irving's letter of Nov. 3, 1917, he identifies
Halstead being in photo of Irving and two other sailors taken at Pensacola
and states that Halstead died and was buried in the south of France. Irving's
diary entry for July 31, 1917, states that Halstead died at Toulon. The nature
of his illness was never revealed.

July 24, 1917 ✧ *Went ashore and visited some English people named Taylor.*

July 25, 1917 ✧ *Practised bomb dropping. Lewis Mch Gun. Shot 25 rounds of Amm.*[12]

July 26, 1917 ✧ *Studied Int. Morse code, wireless operating. Went swimming in the evening.*

July 27, 1917 ✧ *Did quite a bit of Barber Work. Went swimming in the evening.*

July 28, 1917 ✧ *Had my first flight. Alt. 2100 ft. in #80 machine. Hispano-Suiza motor. D.D.*[13] *10:40 to 10:55 with French Pilot named Duhamel. Banquet in evening. A wonderful days experience.*

---

[12]During 1912, U.S. Army Lt. Col. Isaac N. Lewis designed a revolutionary, gas-operated, Infantry-styled, machine gun that was produced in quantity throughout World War I by both British Small Arms of Birmingham, England, and Savage Arms Co. of Utica, N.Y. It saw continuous service within the British Army until 1939. In 1916, B.S.A. stripped the original Mark I Infantry weapon of its rifle stock and heat-dissipating radiator and began production of the Aerial Lewis Machine Gun, Mark II. Further refinements in 1918 produced the final version of this aerial weapon known as the Mark III. The original Infantry version carried 47 rounds of .303 British ammunition in a top-mounted, circular drum having a rate of fire of 500 rounds per minute. Aerial versions increased the capacity of the circular magazine to 97 rounds and the rate of fire to 700 rounds per minute. The Aerial Lewis Machine Gun was considered by many to be the best fully automatic aerial weapon produced during World War I. (Harry Woodman, "Armament Notes No. 2," *Cross and Cockade International Journal* 19, no. 2 [1988])

[13]The DD was the French-built Donnet-Denhaut flying boat powered by the big 180 hp "Hisso" (Hispano-Suiza), carrying a crew of three and later four. Despite the large powerplant, it cruised at a modest 80 mph. The Americans, much to their eventual dislike, were to see a great deal of this "boat" when they began antisubmarine patrols out of the American-operated Naval Air Station at Dunkerque. This station was located just

July 29, 1917 ❖ *Went up to some people to tea named Taylor.*

July 30, 1917 ❖ *Visited some more people to tea. Wrote letter to Lewis.*

American Aviation Corps
St. Raphael Var [?]
France
July 30, 1917

Dear Lewis,-

It has been quite a while since I wrote a letter home but I've wrote two or three and haven't had any answer from them yet. I had a card and a letter from Mamma saying she sent a cake. It was stamped May the 19th I think and I received it July 27.

The cake nearly knocked me over when I opened it for it stunk dreadfully. That was the first mail we received since we left Baltimore. I received a letter and a package from Martha Lester [cousin] last Sunday. The package was a little New Testament. I've been reading quite a lot of it.

Sunday we had a Y.M.C.A. Sunday school meeting and were led by a retired minister, a Rev. Mr. Brown. It was fine and I enjoyed it immensely. He surely give us a good talk.

Well I'll have to tell you how I'm getting along in Aviation. Saturday the 28 of July I had my first *jump*. That is what they call it making a flight *JUMP*. I set in the machine beside the pilot and away we went. It is flying boats, that start off and light on the water. Well, we left the water and started to climb up, up, up, at a speed of about 60 mile an hour. Gosh but it was great. I felt no

---

behind the front lines on the north coast of France. It was put into service by the American Navy under the command of Lt. Chevalier on Jan. 1, 1918, but because of German land and sea shelling and abominable weather conditions it did not begin overwater patrols until spring.

sense of fear whatever. It was so steady that I thought I was riding on a tressel [?]. We rode away out to sea up over the town of St. Raphael, over mountains, and then after we had gained a altitude of 2100 feet we started to spiral down. It was surely great and I am just crazy about it. After Aug. the 6th we will have to take regular flights and have to spend eight hours in the air to qualify. We wig-wag, and also wireless operating. For we have to send messages from the machines while in flight. We also have to practise bomb dropping for this is about the only way to fight submarines. In addition to all this we are getting instruction in operating the Lewis Machine Gun. We shoot about 25 rounds apiece every other day. This is to fight enemy aeroplanes that might attack us.

We have met some Canadian Nurses in a little town about 20 miles away, a place called Cannes. They have treated us fine. We have seen them twice. But its so hard to get liberty leave that we have very little time outside.

We get every other night off and then only till half past nine. Saturday night we had a little banquet in town which we all chipped in an got up. The first good meal since I left Baltimore.

I am doing all the barber work for the bunch and they had a little card of each of us just for a joke. This is the one they had of me. I am enclosing it.[14]

I am making a little extra change on this barber work. I charge one franc for a hair cut and a half franc for a shave. I saved over a hundred dollars so far.

I have passed the examination at Pensacola and received my rating. I am getting forty-four dollars a month now. [See May 1, 1917.]

---

[14]The hand-drawn card in ink of a barber is still in Irving's collection.

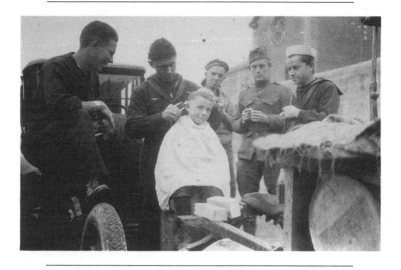

Irving made good pocket money barbering throughout his stint in the Navy. (Courtesy of Roger Sheely)

I am at a loss to know how to send it home and have you put it in the bank for me. I will find out and let you know what I can do about it.

You know that picture I sent you the tall fellow in it has gone crazy and not expected to live. And by the way you don't know how well off you are. For when I tell you that we only get two meals a day and those proportioned out to us it isn't like the United States at all. All we get is Stew and war bread and beans all the time and these are so rotten that I sometimes do without. Believe me I'm much thinner than I was last summer. But thank God I have my health yet. That goes to show what good stock I'm made of.

Such things as Butter, Jam, candy, sugar, milk, tea, Ice Cream, eggs and may other things we don't get at all. And sometimes salt we have to do without. This is the case all over France. So you must not kick if you have to cut out things and live a little cheaper, as Mamma stated she was doing in her letter.[15]

I forgot to tell you that one of our number has been killed already. He fell about 500 ft. and was burned to a crisp. He was buried here in France. It must be something awful for his folks. But this is war and as Sherman put it "War is Hell".

I go swimming in the Mediterranean Sea nearly every night. One of the fellows has a camera and these are a couple of pictures he took. He caught me diving, and by the way I'm getting to be quite a swimmer now. I can float, dive and swim quite a distance.

I wish I had my camera now but I'm afraid to have you send it for it might be sunk by a submarine. I think such might be the case with some of our mail. And by the way don't forget to address my mail to USN 1st Aeronautical Detachment c/o Postmaster, New York.

And it is cheaper for you too as if you addressed it to France it would be extra postage.

I get the New York Herald every day (Paris Edition) and I have cut out a couple of clippings which I will enclose. One is about us being the first Americans to land in France under the Stars and Stripes.

Then there is the description of an air battle giving you an idea of what my work will be.

It seems to be a general anxiousness among all of us to get to the front. But I guess it will come quick enough at that.

Well, I guess I've told you all for this time and I will try

---

[15]The food was so bad at St. Raphael that Navy Doctor Sinton had to order an additional ration of sugar for the Americans.

and write often as it dosen't cost us any postage so I can afford to can't I?

Hoping this finds you all well I am

Your Brother,

Irving

P.S. I am going to take a chance and have you send me a padlock (like cut). You will find it in the lower drawer where we keep our books. Be sure to get one that the keys operate all right. And about the size of the cut I think.

It will only cost a few cents and I will see how long it takes and then I might send for my camera.

July 31, 1917 ✧ *Picking up Morse Code very good now. Went Swimming. Halstead died at Toulon.*

Aug. 1, 1917 ✧ *Wrote a letter to Haskins today. Rained all day.*

Aug. 2, 1917 ✧ *Had neuralgia in my jaw. Didn't sleep a wink all night.*

Aug. 3, 1917 ✧ *Went ashore to Frejus. Tooth still festering. No sleep yet.*

Aug. 4, 1917 ✧ *Went to St. Raphael to Dentist and he fixed it up fine.*

Aug. 5, 1917 ✧ *Went to Cannes. Bathing.* [approx. 30 miles east along the coast from St. Raphael] *Had a picnic in afternoon. Drove Miss Johnson's car.*

Aug. 6, 1917 ✧ *Started in flying. Each were to make four flights and on first flight drop one bomb—small.*

Aug. 7, 1917 ✧ *Second flight 4 bombs—small. Last turn flight 2 large ones. Griffin pilot.*

Aug. 8, 1917 ✧ *Letter from Haze Hammond.* [Hammann. See May 15, 1917]

Aug. 9, 1917 ✧ *Machine slid up on the shore and smashed wings. Pilot unhurt.*

Aug. 10, 1917 ✧ *Went ashore and took my first lesson in French.*

Aug. 11, 1917 ✧ *Payday drawed $52. Went to Frejus to Mdme. Burnel for French lesson with Counts.* [MM2c(A) E. Counts]

Aug. 12, 1917 ✧ *Went in bathing in morning. Went to Frejus in evening.*

Aug. 13, 1917 ✧ *Mail from states. Letter from Lewis and A. Forner.*[16] *Card from Alice.*

Aug. 14, 1917 ✧ *Went to dentist then to bank. Deposited 750F. Went to Frejus in evening and bought a new camera.*

Aug. 15, 1917 ✧ *French Holiday.* [?] *Did about 16 shaves and 10 haircuts. Went to Frejus at night. No flying.*

Aug. 16, 1917 ✧ *Went to St. Raphael. Finished with dentist. Paid him 10 francs. Bailey and I bought a French camera from him. No flying today.* [Landsman for Quartermaster (Air) D. F. Bailey]

Aug. 17, 1917 ✧ *Machine fell first thing in the morning. Pilot killed in a F.B.A.*[17] *Buried Sunday.*

---

[16] Andrew Forner, maternal uncle.

[17] F.B.A. (Franco British Aviation), a consortium, built a series of open, two-place, bi-wing flying boats for patrol and light bombing use. Used primarily by France, the series B was powered by a 100 hp Gnome rotary, the C by a 130 hp Clerget Rotary, and the H series with the V-8, liquid-cooled, 170 hp Hispano-Suiza. The F.B.A. series was the most extensively built flying boats of World War I. (Heinz J. Nowarra, *Marine Aircraft of the 1914–1918 War* [Letchworth, England: Harleyford Publ., 1966])

Aug. 18, 1917 ✧ *First flight with Lt. Griffin in F.B.A. G4. Dropped 4 bombs. Made very good hits. Time 9:05 to 9:50 A.M. Another machine fell. Two killed. One a watery grave.*

Aug. 19, 1917 ✧ *Stayed home. Had my hair clipped. Went to Frejus in evening.*

Aug. 20, 1917 ✧ *Started to take pictures with new camera. Worked fine.*

Aug. 21, 1917 ✧ *Did a lot of barber work. Took three pictures. Griffin flying every day with us dropping bombs.*

Aug. 22, 1917 ✧ *Worked with Bailey in dark room developing. Took half a dozen more plates.*

1st Aeronautic Detachment
c/o Post master New York City
Aug. 22, 1917

Dear Lewis,–

Received both your letters one last week and one today and also Mamma's. I have had a great deal of mail lately and I am simply swamped. It will take me a week to catch up with my correspondence.

I received a letter from H. Warren saying they sent me a package. Also that Shrieves were sending me a package. I received the one from Warren but none from Shrieves yet.

It was a lot of junk. Some I can use and some I'll have to give away. The most useful thing in it was a towel and a cake of soap. But it cost something like a dollar to send. You see it was returned and they sent it again as first class mail. I think they have changed the P. Post system now, permitting American Soldiers in France to send and receive most anything.

I wish my friends would not send me anything for if they

could imagine me trying to move around France and nothing but a bag (about the size of a brand sack)[18] to pack my duds and stuff in they wouldn't wonder why I say this. I'll have to withdraw some of that for I wouldn't have cared if it had been candy or chocolat. If you can imagine being without a bit of sweet stuff for nearly three months. Bitter coffee and such things. It makes you hanker for sweet as you do for salt.

Mamma spoke about she would like to send me some cake or doughnuts. She ought to know that I don't care for cake and besides its impossible to keep long enough to come over here.

I am flying nearly every day now and getting so used to it that I don't pay any attention to it any more. Just go out and jump in the machine as I used to jump on the motorcycle and take a ride.

I am sorry to say that another of our fellows has been killed. He and a Frenchman collided in the air. The Frenchman landed safely but he tumbled and fractured his skull.

There has been several Frenchmen killed since I've been here. I think its due mostly to carelessness.

One was killed Tuesday and two on Wednesday so we had three Frenchmen and one American this week.

I don't know as I ought to mention these things but their [sic] bound to happen just the same as you pick up the paper Monday morning and read of the Automobile accidents. It isn't any different and almost always due to carelessness.

We fly in the morning and that leaves most of the afternoon to ourselves and this is the time I use to do my barber work. Believe me I'm getting all I can handle to. Just to show you what I did on Saturday I cut twelve haircuts and shaved twenty men.

---

[18]By "brand sack" he probably means a cloth sack in which grain, or bran, is carried. He is referring to his "Sea Bag."

I've got it right down to a science now. My average work is two or three hair cuts and five or six shaves a day.[19]

My pay has been increased to fifty two dollars a month now, and since we have been flying we get a fifty percent increase which amounts to seventy eight dollars a month. I haven't drawen this yet but expect to the next pay day. I am putting my money in the bank and will decide later what I'll do with it.

Next Tuesday we leave here and go to our own station at Bordeaux.[20] I'll miss the salt water bathing for I've been going in every day I've been here. I can swim like a fish and dive like a frog now and I think this swimming has helped my health along for I feel like a fellow fifteen years old.

You asked me about fishing. I haven't been able to do any yet. There doesn't seem to be any one interested in it here.

I hope you'll be sure to dry out the line and the hooks before you put them away and use the tackle all you want only take care of it as I would if I were using it. Thanks very much for looking after my hunting clothing.

---

[19]During the depression days of the thirties, my Dad, Irving's brother Frank, did his best to stretch every dime by taking me to Uncle Irving's for a free haircut. Uncle Irving used hand-operated clippers, probably the ones he bought in France, and once in a while they would pull my hair instead of cut it and I would yelp and jump. Uncle Irving would holler, "Hold Still!" and I would become frightened and intimidated. It took only a few of those sessions before my dear Dad found the necessary coins to send his son to a barber who used electric clippers.

[20]Irving was actually going beyond Bordeaux to the shores of Lake Lacanau located very close to the west coast of France. This site is approx. 175 air miles south of St. Nazaire where the USS *Neptune* put him ashore just three months previously. There, Irving and others from St. Raphael would literally hack out of a pine forest the Navy's most significant seaplane pilot and ground training base in the Europe of World War I. Irving's future combat pilot, Kenneth MacLeish, and most of the other Navy pilots of heavier-than-air craft would pass through Moutchic.

If you find time I wish you would look over the guns and rifles and see that they are not rusting and oil them up a bit.

I think you are doing fine at the A.L.Co. Was that $40.00 for two weeks?

Are you using the slide rule I made and how do you like it?

Tell Johnny DeGroff[21] that I said it wouldn't do to take a spill like that when your flying an aeroplane because you wouldn't get out of it as easy as just loosing a little hide.

I told Perry[21] that I would write to him but I don't think I'll start any more correspondence just yet for I can't handle what I've got right now. Tell him for me that I am making a flight every morning and its much better than scrubbing tracings and seeing how near you can come to the cuspidor with a mouth full of tobacco juice.

Is Foulder[21] on the draft list? I don't think he thought very much of my enlisting but you tell him that when the government sends him over here to dig in the trenches I'll drop a bottle of champagne out of my aeroplane for him. Ha. Ha.

Tell Gus[21] that he might as well break off chewing for when he gets over here he won't be able to get any tobacco.

I wish you could tell me about this mail. I don't put any stamps on it for the French government allows us Free mail and if you have to pay postage over there on my mail I think its a rotten shame. For if the French can afford to do this the American government surely ought to.

One of our French pilots sunk a submarine the other day. Its a wonder too for they seem to be awful slow. It won't be long before I will be writing and telling you that I have just come back from a flight and successfully sinking one.

---

[21]Co-workers at the American Locomotive Co.

Its just the same as shooting at a target. You look over the sights, keep your machine horizontal in flight, draw a fine bead, pull the spring and the bomb falls.

It explodes about 8 feet under water. It dosen't [*sic*] have to drop exactly on the sub but as near as possible. If it is within fifty feet it will destroy a submarine or sink it.

I am enclosing a couple of pictures one of our detachment and one of myself as I look as an aviator.

It was snapped by one of the fellows just before I started out on a flight. It isn't very clear but I think you can recognize who it is. I have had my hair clipped off. It was falling out so fast that I surely begin to think I was going to be bald. It will give it a rest and besides it is much cooler.

I see by the paper that it is pretty hot over there. Its the same here only the nights are cool. I hope the climate is as good as it is here at Bordeaux.

I wrote to Mamma about two weeks ago and I told quite a lot so I think I'll close hoping this finds you all well. I am,

Your Brother,

Irving

Will write when I get to our new base.

Watch and tell me if my mail is censored.

Yours reaches me unopened.

If you write Military Service in the corner of the envelope I don't think you will have to put any stamp on them.

Aug. 23, 1917 ✧ Second flight with Griffin 8:36 to 8:45 F.B.A. G10. Hispano-Suiza motor. Dropped two bombs. Word from Tours that Manley killed.

Aug. 24, 1917 ✧ Big day barber work. Getting ready to move. Went to St. Raphael in evening.

U.S. Naval Aviation Petty Officer Sheely dressed in 1917-style flying leather (Courtesy of Roger Sheely)

[facing page, bottom] *Men at French Naval Air Station at St. Raphael. Irving wrote on the back: "This is our little detachment of 50 aviators whom are the only people I've talked to in over three months. You see I can't foly this French jolip good enough to have a conversation with a Frenchman. There is another detachment of 50 at Tours (near Paris) studying aviation. Can you find me? [third row from front, third in from right] The man in officer's uniform is Lieutenant Griffin [Lt. Virgil C. Griffin, Naval Aviator #41) who is a very good pilot. The two beside him are Chief Stone and Chief Leonhardt who are our immediate bosses." (Courtesy of Roger Sheely)*

Petty Officer Sheely aboard a French Donnet-Denhaut flying boat at St. Raphael (Courtesy of Roger Sheely)

Aug. 25, 1917 ✧ *Last day flying at St. Raphael. Went to town in evening.*

Aug. 26, 1917 ✧ *Stayed at barracks all day packing up. News that Manley was killed at Tours.*[22]

Aug. 27, 1917 ✧ *Our baggage left about noon and we all slept at St. Raphael. I slept in the Terminus Hotel.*

Aug. 28, 1917 ✧ *Left St. R. at 4 A.M. Passed through Marseille. Rode all day and all night.*

---

[22]Landsman for Quartermaster (Air) G. H. Manley came over with the First Aeronautical Detachment on the USS *Neptune*. During his three months at St. Raphael, Irving mentions four of his Pensacola comrades killed in flight training plus the death of Halstead from bizarre symptoms.

CHAPTER 3

Moutchic

August 29 to November 10, 1917

Aug. 29, 1917 ✧ *Arrived in Bordeaux Wed. morning about 11 A.M. Left B. at about 5 P.M. and arrived at Moutchic at 7:30 P.M.*[1]

Aug. 30, 1917 ✧ *Put flooring in our tents. Built the mess hall and got things very well settled.*

Aug. 31, 1917 ✧ *Started to dig a well. Struck water and had to leave it unfinished.*

Sept. 1, 1917 ✧ *Fixed up a dark room with Bailey. Went in bathing. Water cold. Shaved my head.*

Sept. 2, 1917 ✧ *Call for volunteers at 8 o'clock and on our way at 9 all packed. Arrive at Cazaux at about 4 P.M.*[2]

---

[1]On Aug. 31, 1917, NAS Moutchic began operation as a flight and ground training station in France. It was constructed under command of Lt. John Lansing Callan of Albany, N.Y., a street neighbor and an acquaintance of Irving's family. Callan had been taught to fly by Glen Curtiss at Hammondsport, N.Y., became a pilot for the Curtiss Aviation Co., and regularly flew over Albany. (Noel Shirley, "John Lansing Callan—Naval Aviation Pioneer," *Over The Front Journal* [League of WWI Aviation Historians] Vol. 2, No. 2 [1987]: 180-85)

[2]Cazeaux, a French aerial gunnery training school about 35 miles south of Moutchic.

Sept. 3, 1917 ✧ *Target practise with 22 and .303 carbine and mch. gun. 8 shots at target from aeroplane. First flight in a Farman #9.*[3] *French pilot.*

Sept. 4, 1917 ✧ *Made another flight, also a ride on the glider firing from all.*[4]

Sept. 5, 1917 ✧ *Shooting from aeroplane again, also from motor boat. Shooting at trap with shotguns. Right at home with the old gun.*

Sept. 6, 1917 ✧ *Friday flying again. Shooting at balloons with carbine .303.*

Sept. 8, 1917 ✧ *Made another flight and all kinds of shooting, traps, carbines, mch. guns.*

Sept. 9, 1917 ✧ *Another flight in morning firing with mch. gun. Picked black berries for supper.*

Sept. 10, 1917 ✧ *Made two flights today shooting with mch. gun, one in the morning, one in the afternoon.*

---

[3]The Farman was a popular French biplane with a short fuselage mounted between the upper and lower wings. This fuselage contained two cockpits and an 80 hp Gnome rotary engine. The pusher propeller rotated between four structural members that went back to the tailplanes. The observer sat in the forward cockpit ahead of the wings enabling him to see, photograph, or fire a machine gun in a 180-degree arc. This feature was very useful before the advent of synchronized fire through a tractor-mounted engine and propeller. They were used on the western front only throughout 1914–1915, being too underpowered to carry a Lewis machine gun above 3,500 ft. (O. G. Thetford, comp., *Aircraft of the 1914–1918 War,* edited by D. A. Russell [Letchworth, England: Harleyford Publ., 1954], p. 103)

[4]Irving definitely wrote, "also a *ride on* the glider firing from all." Speculation suggests that after a practice gunnery flight, he then had a *ride on* something that "glided" along the ground, possibly on rails, providing another and perhaps simpler means for the student to practice firing from a moving platform.

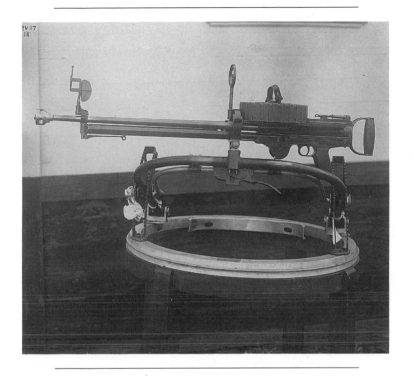

Single Mark III aerial Lewis machine gun with Norman vane front sight on Scarff ring mount as used in observer position of such aircraft as DH-4, DH-9, and DH-9A, Breguet and Donnet-Denhaut flying boats (Courtesy of Roger Sheely)

Sept. 11, 1917 ❖ *Payday drawed 295 Francs. Made another flight. Started on French rations. Brady joined us in Lipsey's place.*

Sept. 12, 1917 ❖ *Motor boat shooting. Vickers and Lewis mch. gun instruction. No flying today.*

Sept. 13, 1917 ❖ *Examined in shooting deflection, trap shooting and six millimeter. Made a flight in F.B.A.*

Sept. 14, 1917 ❖ *Flying again, same routine over again nearly every day. Mail from Lewis.*

Sept. 15, 1917 ❖ *More flying. Shot at target (Maggie).[5] Made a score of 8 hits and 11 points.*

Sept. 16, 1917 ❖ *Shooting, and all kinds of it. 6 millimeter, .303 carbines, Lewis mch. guns and Colts.*

1st Aeronautic Detachment U.S. Navy
23 Rue De Paix Paris
France
Sept. 16, 1917

Dear Alice,-

I think I received a letter from you while I was yet at St. Raphael and so I think I will address this one to you. I know all of you read them and so it dosen't make much difference. I received a letter from Lewis yesterday and I will try and answer it

---

[5]"Maggie" and references to her apparel such as "Maggie's Drawers," a flag waved from the target pit to inform the shooter that he missed the target, have long been heard around a target range. In this instance "Maggie" herself suggests an oversize, perhaps air-towed, aerial gunnery target. Later references to firing at Maggie and sausage targets from the air lend some support to this speculation.

in this. You see I am not on this earth long enough to do as much as I want to. I mean this as a little joke, but I will explain.

Most of the time I am up among the clouds and the time I am on the ground I am either sleeping or eating.

I have to be on the job at a quarter of seven and I lay in till the last minute and hardly give myself time to eat breakfast. Then I am off in the air till about eleven. I eat dinner and am off again till seven o'clock.

Some days I don't fly and then I am shooting with the Lewis Machine gun. We also have the Vickers Mch. gun but we use the Lewis in aviation.

I have done a lot of shooting from a machine (aeroplane) at a target on the water. We shoot from a height of about 200 meters.

Next week I expect to do some shooting at a (what we call a war sausage).

They tow a sausage shape bag around with an aeroplane and we shoot at it from another aeroplane. Sounds like a lot of Bluff don't it?

I forgot to tell you where I am. Way over in the western part of France now. And we are getting much better chow too.

My mail has to go through Paris so that's why I give you this address.[6] Do you have to pay postage on the letters I send you? I have been writing quite a few letters to the states and I haven't put any stamps on them. By the way this mail has to be censored before I seal it so that's the reason I have to be careful what I tell you and where I am located.

Two weeks from now, when we get through with this place,

---

[6] This explains why many of Irving's letters are headlined Paris when he is actually elsewhere in France. Paris is the location of U.S. Naval Aviation headquarters in Europe.

we move again, where, I don't know. It might be the Front, or America, for all I know.

All I care now is that we get half way decent grub and a place to sleep and I feel alright.

Lewis said that he found a new place to fish. Hope he leaves a few till I get back. Yes, I know where Milton is. I've been there. Guess there isn't many places I haven't been around Albany, is there?

How would it seem to you if I came sailing over Albany in an aeroplane. Before I enlisted I would have thought this quite a big thing but now after I've done so much flying I think of it as a mere trifle.

My commanding officer is a fellow from my own town. He lives on Clinton Ave. about #100 I think. His father is a real estate man. You will have to guess his name as I am not permitted to write it here. He was sure glad to see me. I remember seeing him fly at Maple Beach Park a long time ago. [Lt. John L. Callan]

Well, I think I will close as I have told all I can think of. Hoping this finds you all well, I am,

Your Brother,

Irving

P.S. I think I have received all of your letters and I try to answer them as soon as I can. I can't write a letter to each one of you, all at once for I would have to write the same thing over again.

You see what I mean is that this letter although being addressed to Alice answers all of this too.

In my last letter I sent a picture of myself in an aeroplane at St. Raphael. Did you get it?

To Lewis—Take a run over my guns especially the .351 Winchester and run a cleaning rod through it soaked in oil, and oil all up a bit to keep them from rusting.

Merci beaucoup

Sept. 17, 1917 ✧ *Shooting at balloons with .303 carbines. Shooting at the trap.*

Sept. 18, 1917 ✧ *Grub is very good at Cazaux. Sorry it is going to end this week. Flying. Shot at Maggie.*

Sept. 19, 1917 ✧ *Flying again. Result with Maggie turned me out first. Wrote some letters home.*

Sept. 20, 1917 ✧ *Flying and shooting with machine guns. Motor boat shooting. Arrival of new Navy Officer from Paris.*

Sept. 21, 1917 ✧ *No flying or motor boats. Station out of gas.*

Sept. 22, 1917 ✧ *Examinations in 6 mm. Got 80. In .303 carbine got 39. Lewis mch. gun got 16 and finished with jams on Vickers, Lewis & Winchester.*

Sept. 23, 1917 ✧ *Went up 4000 ft. and shot at the sausage. Caudron machine. First flight in land machine.[7]*

Sept. 24, 1917 ✧ *[Irving's 24th birthday] Getting ready to leave again. All through with examinations. Left for Moutchic again.*

Sept. 25, 1917 ✧ *The boys have one hangar up and we helped put up the second one. Started to erect two F.B.A. machines #295 and #296.*

Sept. 26, 1917 ✧ *Did quite a lot of swimming.*

Sept. 27, 1917 ✧ *Caught some perch on a set line. Finished on the planes.*

---

[7]Two-place training plane with a fuselage only as long as the wings were wide. The "tail feathers" were attached by flimsy structural members reaching back to them. This same unusual aircraft was used to train the rookie Navy pilot candidates at Tours.

[*On September 27, 1917, Ens. Robert A. Lovett (later Sec. Def.) made the first flight at NAS Moutchic, France, in an F.B.A. seaplane, the assembly of which had been under his direction. He was a member of the First Yale Unit, a volunteer group of Yale students who privately taught themselves to fly and were then commissioned as Naval aviators. (Van Wyen, "Naval Aviation," p. 33)*]

Sept. 28, 1917 ✧ *Worked on the small stores. Went swimming too. Caught some more fish.*

Sept. 29, 1917 ✧ *Went to Bordeaux on the first train. Walked all over the town. Also rode on the street car. Could ride for one cent anywhere.*

Sept. 30, 1917 ✧ *Put 300 francs in the bank on Saturday.*

Oct. 1, 1917 ✧ *Worked in Callan's quarters. Went swimming.*

Oct. 2, 1917 ✧ *Washed some clothes.*

Oct. 3, 1917 ✧ *Started to erect two F.B.A. seaplanes #297 and #298. Moved the boxes down to the hanger.*

1st Aeronautical Detachment
23 Rue De La Paix
Paris, France
Oct. 3, 1917

Dear Lewis

Received your letter a couple of days ago and also Mamma's with it.

The pictures are fine. I wish I had my Ansco vest pocket here but I'm afraid to take a chance on having it sent across.

By the way I haven't received the package yet but hope to soon. I wish you hadn't bothered to send it. Please don't send anything without my asking for it. We are very well supplied with heavy clothing. In fact we are not allowed to wear anything that is non-regulation.

We are living in tents again and we are getting American grub and its much better. I am feeling fine too. Flying seems to agree with me very much, but I haven't been doing much the last week.

Last Saturday I went to Bordeaux and stayed till Sunday. Had a dandy time. Met a lot of soldiers from the west coast (California). They were glad to see us. It was the first liberty (overnight) that I had since I left the U.S.

A week ago Sunday I made my highest flight. I went up 4000 feet. This isn't very high but when you are up there it seems like a duest of a ways down. did you get my picture I sent you?

I see you are getting to be quite a fisherman. I have caught a few perch and bull-heads on a set line since I've been here.

Guess I'm going to miss my fall hunting this year. By the way it started the first of October to, didn't it? Well, I guess I'll save my money for a good big hunt when I get back.

I have saved one thousand and fifty francs so far. Wish it was dollars.

I have it in a bank at Bordeaux.

I have answered all the letters of those you spoke of. The ones who sent me packages. I received all the five letters you sent me.

When I write to you I answer any of the letters from home. Mean this answers Mamma's as well as yours. Me comprevou vous. Darn it! I get all balled up on this French junk.

I have been writing to a French girl at St. Raphael in English and she writes to me in French. I have the darndest time reading it you ever saw. Well, I suppose thats the only way to learn it anyway.

Guess this will be all for this time hoping this finds you all well, I am

Your brother

Irving

P.S. I will write again as soon as I get the package.

Oct. 4, 1917 ✧ *Went fishing after supper. Caught some bullheads and perch.*

Oct. 5, 1917 ✧ *Finished the hanger and put the machines in it.*

Oct. 6, 1917 ✧ *We have five machines now and things are getting very well started.*

Oct. 7 & 8, 1917 ✧ *Stayed in camp all day. Wrote some letters. All mail is censored at our camp and couldn't write very much what was going on.*

Oct. 9, 1917 ✧ *My first watch in truck. Spent all night with the stars for a roof. Seemed rather queer.*[8]

Oct. 10, 1917 ✧ *Changed our mess hall. Made it out of aeroplane boxes.*

Oct. 11, 1917 ✧ *Worked a little on the dark room today. Chow is much better now and feeling fine. On watch tonight from 8 to 10.*

Oct. 12, 1917 ✧ *Started to do the barber work for the camp at Moutchic. Callen gave me three half days a week to do it.*

---

[8]A careful reader may have difficulty with this entry. The reference to the stars may appear in conflict with the two weeks of rain cited in the next letter, but perhaps actually seeing stars above that one night out of those two weeks was what made it seem "rather queer."

Oct. 13, 1917 ✧ *Some ambulance men arrived and joined our Detachment.*

Oct. 14, 1917 ✧ *Our YMCA building is partly up. another hanger is started.*

1st Aeronautic Detachment
23 Rue De La Paix
Paris, France
Oct. 14, 1917

Somewhere in France

Dear George [friend],-

I have just received your interesting and most welcome letter tonight and as I have a little time before the bugle sounds, for lights out, I am going to try and answer it.

Today is the first the sun has shown for 14 days and it has rained day and night all that time. We sleep in tents and the water has come through the fly dripped on the tent and soaked through everything. My bunk is cold and wet yet from it.

But I don't mind all this. I get up in the morning, put my head through the flap, smile a little bit perhaps as I call my tent mate [D. F. Bailey] and tell him, "Get up old scout we're going to have lots of weather outside today". He will rub his eyes and say to me, "What do you mean old man, is it raining again?". Yes, George, I've been flying quite a lot, been up to a height of four thousand feet and feel just as easy and unconcerned as if I were riding a motorcycle up Clinton Ave.

There is no great sensation to it as one would think. Of course you can see a great ways off.

Looking down from this height a man looks like a speck and you have to look sharp to see him then. Roads and rivers look like thread lines.

In your letter you asked if I found the comfort kit useful. Yes, it comes in handy real often. But to tell you the truth I have enough thread and needles already to last me my whole enlistment.

I am in immediate need of nothing at best that I can think of now. But if they insist on doing something for us "fellers in France" we could accept with many thanks and smiles some smokes or chocolate. Chocolate we get over here is full of grit and its awful bitter, besides being very expensive. For a bar that one would pay 10 cents in the states we have to pay 1 franc and a half and two francs.

Please don't take it that I am asking for this, George. I'm only taking the precaution so you won't send me another sewing kit.

You asked me if I am supplied with a testament. Yes, I have three of them. One very nice one, pocket size, Morocco bound, the others are cloth bound.

I am trying to read them every day but I have so much letter writing to do and such short hours between taps that I don't get to read all I would like to.

But I know Christ will help me in everything I do and will be with me wherever I go.

He has done for me everything I have asked of him that he has saw fit for me to have. I am healthy, strong and happy and if the time comes when I am in great dangers I will meet them unflinching. I don't fear battle, on the contrary am anxious to be getting into action.

I have had all kind of instruction in fighting in the air. Machine gun practise and also bomb dropping. I am just itching to get at those submarines and see if we can't stop some of this ruthless warfare.

George, if you will do me a favor by showing this letter to your father, whom I owe a letter to, it will save me this extra writing.

66

Maybe I can get to write a little oftener in that way. Our mail is all censored so I can't write everything I'd like to. Hoping to hear from you again I remain

Your friend
Irving

Oct. 15, 1917 ✧ *Mornings are very cold now and its rather tuff crawling out in the morning.*

Oct. 16, 1917 ✧ *Callen asked about the Dark Room and how I was coming along with it.*

Oct. 17, 1917 ✧ *Worked on #807 FBA and erected it complete. Took 5 exposures with Owens camera.*

Oct. 18, 1917 ✧ *Worked on hanger. Finished it. Did barber work all afternoon. Cut Callen's hair.*

Oct. 19, 1917 ✧ *Word that pilots from St. Raphael are coming to join us.*

Oct. 20, 1917 ✧ *Made addition on the mess hall. Chow continues to be fine. Received package from home. Contained candy, cake, gum, jelly and chocolate.*

Oct. 21, 1917 ✧ *Tent inspection. Took two exposures of it with French camera. Wrote some letters to the folks and friends in states.*

1st Aeronautic Detachment
23 Rue De La Paix
Paris, France
Oct. 21, 1917

Dear Lewis

Received your letter of the 16 inst and also the package yesterday. By Golly! but there was some charges on it, wasn't there? Well it tasted pretty good too. Tell Andy[9] and Mr. Smith I am very thankful to them for their part in it. Everything was all right in it except the cake which was really dried up. I don't care for cake very much so that diden't make so much difference. My tent partner takes a crack at it once in a while with me and in this way I guess we won't have to waste it.

I guess I told you I wrote to Warrens and Shrieves and thanked them for the things they sent me.

If any more of those packages come through I'll start up a sewing school and close up my barber shop.

Thanks for cleaning up the guns. I wish you had run a rag through the 351 Winchester and then run another through it soaked with oil. I thought I told you I sold the Remington pump. Yes, a fellow up in Barberville bought it. He was out hunting with me, took a fancy to it and wanted to buy it. I sold it to him for twenty one dollars.

You surely made some dough at the A.L.Co. this summer. I hope Frank is making good and sticks to it. Even if he dosen't advance at the A.L.Co. he is getting the experience. Believe me my experience has helped me at the A.L.Co. and the Times Union for I learned a lot about motors with the T.U. and drafting will help me in Aerial Navigation and other things.

You asked me about Lasher from Union College.[10] Yes, he is with us. There are a couple of others from home here too. I

---

[9]Andrew Gregg, fiancé of Irving's sister, Laura.

[10]Herbert Lasher, member of First Aeronautical Detachment. Came over on the USS *Jupiter* and received pilot training and French brevet as pilot at Tours. Later to be commissioned and made Naval Aviator #763. Union College Schenectady, N.Y. BSEE, Class of 1917. Died Nov. 28, 1972. See May 6, 1918, for near fatal flying accident at NAS Dunkerque. (Herbert Lasher, Letter[s] written to L. Sheely)

haven't got time to write to Gus and Perry for I have all the correspondence I can handle now. Just tell them for me I have done lots of flying and expect to do a lot more before I get back.

I got a letter from Scottie [11] a couple of days ago saying he was sending some smokes and chocolate. I haven't received them as yet. Scottie is a great old scout. I wish I had a couple of fellows like him with me over here.

Well its nearly seven months I've been in the service. Doesn't seem that long though. All I have is three years and a butt to do yet.[12] Hope this old war is over by that time.

Our life here seems a lot like camp life I've done in the north woods. Our meals are cooked over a fire on the ground. we sleep in tents, bathe in the lake [Lacanau] and wash our own clothes.

Our spare time is devoted to baseball, football, writing letters, reading, sometimes sewing (this only when absolutely necessary to avoid exposure).

We go to bed with the chickens and outside of this we have a hell of a fine time. Guess I won't know how to live in civil life after this or how it will feel to have to wear a collar again.

Well so long for this time

Sincerely

Irving

Oct. 22, 1917 ✦ *Rained all day. Bought a raincoat from Hockett. Paid him 60 francs for it.*

Oct. 23, 1917 ✦ *Diechman took charge of camp.* [Lt. Grattan C. Dichman Naval Aviator #30 replaced Lt. Callan]

---

[11]Scott Walrath, a Masonic Brother and close friend.

[12]Irving's metaphor was clear to him. After a couple of puffs, there was nothing much that was shorter than a Bull-Durham cigarette "butt."

Oct. 24, 1917 ✧ *Hangars were assigned to Pilots and M.Mates. I am in the First Esquadrille* [Squadron], *second section as second Mechanician.*

[*"Routine instruction in flight and ground courses began at NAS Moutchic, France on Oct. 24, 1917. It was now the main training station serving naval air units in Europe." ("United States Naval Aviation 1910–1970," p. 29)*]

Oct. 25, 1917 ✧ *Finished the YMCA and moved the barbershop in it.*

Oct. 26, 1917 ✧ *Worked in the hanger. Kneip and detail of Observers left for La Croix* [NAS Le Croisic provided aerial escort for incoming ship convoys from the west.] *These men were the first assigned to a permanent station.*

{ *"Two members of the First Aeronautical Detachment, Weddell, pilot, and Eddy Kneip, observer, were killed at Le Croisic. Returning from patrol one afternoon in a Tellier [French flying boat], Weddell put the ship in a tight turn before landing and a wing crumbled. They crashed in the bay just off the station" (Van Wyen, "Naval Aviation," p. 13). This occurred some time after November 22, 1917, when the first armed USN aviation patrol was made over the Atlantic Ocean ("United States Naval Aviation 1910–1970," p. 30).*}

Oct. 27, 1917 ✧ *Bailey left me the plates and I decided to do some developing and printing myself.*

Oct. 28, 1917 ✧ *Felt rather homesick to lose my tent partner.*

Oct. 29, 1917 ✧ *Went to Bordeaux to have my teeth fixed. Bought some paper, tanks and equipment to do some photography work.*

Oct. 30, 1917 ❖ Went up with Lieut. Lovett to take some pictures but had some engine trouble and had to come down.

Oct. 31, 1917 ❖ Payday drawed 470 Francs. This included my 50%.

Nov. 1, 1917 ❖ Made a stove out of some tin cans for our tent. [See letter of Nov. 3, 1917]

Nov. 2, 1917 ❖ Flew with Parker three times today.[13]

Nov. 3, 1917 ❖ Busy all day changing our mess hall. Making it bigger for our boys who joined us from Pensacola and Brest.

---

23 Rue De La Paix
Paris, France
Nov. 3, 1917
Somewhere in France

Dear Laura,-

Received the package you sent me a couple of days ago and your letter dated Oct. 3 today. I also received a card from Mamma and a letter dated Sept. 30 from Lewis this week.

Lewis told me to acknowledge these letters by dates so you see I am trying to carry out his instructions. However, I think its a very good plan.

I was very glad to get the things you sent me especially the *Milk Chocalates* the first I've tasted in six months.

Its started to get cold here and its rained a great deal of the time so I think I'll begin to use the sweater. It will come in handy when I stand watches at night.

I wrote to Lewis a couple of weeks ago and I told him that I

---

[13]Probably Erlon "Pete" Parker, N.A. #758. Crossed with First Aeronautical Detachment on USS *Jupiter.*

had received the box of foodstuffs. Guess what I've made out of the box. Well I gathered some milk cans and made a stove pipe and used the box as a stove. It works swell and believe me it feels good in my tent these cold nights.

Before this I have been sleeping with my heavy underwear and sometimes with my socks and hat on to keep warm. But since I've made the stove I am sleeping in my *Bear* skin again.

I haven't done much flying this past month. We have moved again and we are getting a station ready. I have charge of two aeroplanes which I fly in and have to take care of.

I am getting so used to flying that I think no more of it that I did of riding a motorcycle.

In fact there is more sensation in riding a good speedy motorcycle than there is in flying anyway.

I guess half the mail I have sent gets sunk. I wrote a letter to Mamma and sent some pictures of myself in a bathing suit swimming in the Mediterranean Sea. Also a picture of diving off a pier. And you diden't receive it?

I don't see why you have to pay postage on the letters for we have received official instructions that all Soldiers and Sailors on active service in France can send mail to the U.S. free. You asked me about that fellow on that picture post card. He died a long time ago and is buried in the southern part of France. [Halstead. The photo of the three men in Navy blue taken at Pensacola.]

You also spoke about some fellows who would like to receive mail. Yes, there is a lot of them that would like to receive it but are too lazy to answer letters. Like myself for instance. I've got about a dozen letters to write.

I am going to drop a line to that Mr. Clark of Kinderhook that Lewis spoke about. He is a fine fellow and I had quite a time with him when I was working on the Times-Union job. I stayed overnight with him. He is principal of the Kinderhook High

School. I guess there is a few hundred more people in the vicinity of Albany that know me just from that T.U. job.

So you come near getting hooked up, did you? And threw it over your shoulder, Eh! Well, I'll be "Gosh Blamed". Guess I'll hook on to one of these French girls. I haven't heard from Olive in a long time. Maybe she is on the way over here though. She said she had joined some Red Cross arrangement. What ever that is.

Before I forget it I wanted to tell Mamma that I have made out an allotment of forty dollars a month starting with the month of November. I would like her to pay my bills such as insurance and lodge dues and put the rest in the bank for me. If she needs any of it to go ahead and use it. Last month I drawed eighty two dollars for the month of October.

I have saved over fifteen hundred francs and have a bank account in Bordeaux. Barber work gives me all the spending money I need so you see I am getting along nicely. I have bought a French camera. It takes a picture 9 by 12 centimeters [approx. 3.5" x 4.75"]. It is one of these plate cameras. I bought it at a bargain second hand and it takes swell pictures.

Have you used that roll that I sent back. If you haven't I wish you would try it out. Do you know how to work it?

We have a YMCA building now and they have a piano and a victrola with it. Its just a portable building but we have some good times in it. Once in a while we have some boxing matches in it.[14]

One night they got me to put the gloves on with another fellow. Well, I diden't know much about boxing and conse-

---

[14]On April 6, 1917, John R. Mott, General Secretary of the International YMCA Committee, wired President Wilson volunteering "the full service of

quently I got hit a couple of times on the nose and once on the lip.

Well, my nose started to bleed and my lip swelled up so I give up boxing for good.

I like to see someone else do it. Anyway it don't hurt so much when you see the other fellow get hit.

If you should happen to be sending anything to me again I wish you would put a pair of goggles in with it. The pair I want is in the top drawer in the red bureau in our room. It only has one lenze [sic] in it. Just take the glass out by breaking it and send me the frame. I suppose you wonder why I want the frame only. Well, in flying the air passes around this pocket formed by the frame and dosen't make your eyes water. This is the shape of the lenze on the pair I want.[15]

Well, so long for this time, I remain

Your Brother,

Irving

---

the Association." The government asked the YMCA to take responsibility for canteen operation. To meet this obligation, the YMCA raised more than $15,000,000 and mobilized nearly 2,600 secretaries (volunteers). To supply the canteens of France, the YMCA imported flour and sugar and established "factories" to make candy, jam, and biscuits, churning out 10,160,000 packages. The secretaries carried cigarettes to the front. They showed movies in leave areas and wrote letters for wounded or sick soldiers. In France the work comprised the erection and equipment of 491 wooden "huts" and 1,045 tents and their effective operation at a total cost of $12,336,800. (Andrea Hinding, *Proud Heritage: A History in Pictures of the YMCA in the United States* [Virginia Beach: Donning Co., 1988], p. 97; C. H. Hopkins, *History of the Y.M.C.A. in North America* [Association Press, 1951], p. 490)

[15]Here Irving makes a sketch of the goggles. Note the amount of things he has had to supply himself and doesn't seem to think it unusual.

Nov. 4, 1917 ✧ *My allotment started.*

Nov. 5, 1917 ✧ *I was appointed second Mechanician on machines #297 and #807.*

Nov. 6, 1917 ✧ *Mr. Lovett took me up to take some pictures of our station at Moutchic.*

Nov. 7, 1917 ✧ *Word that the pilots were to go to the acrobatic training school.*

Nov. 8, 1917 ✧ *Did barber work all day because it rained and there was no flying.*

Nov. 9, 1917 ✧ *At 12 o'clock Lieut. Lovett informed me that I was to go to Dunkirk. Maybe I wasn't surprised.*

Nov. 10, 1917 ✧ *Left Moutchic in the morning and changed at Bordeaux. Left Bordeaux at 8:25 PM for Paris.*

CHAPTER 4

England

November 11, 1917 to March 2, 1918

Nov. 11, 1917 ✧ *Rode all night and arrived [Paris] in the morning. Met Kinnie at the YMCA and put up there.*[1]

Nov. 12, 1917 ✧ *Went to headquarters and saw Gallivan and Duffy.*[2]

Nov. 12, 1917

Dear Lewis,-

I am in Paris tonight on my way to the front.[3] Thought I would drop you a line to let you know.

We leave tomorrow morning. I am stopping at the YMCA overnight.

Our orders to go were rather sudden but I expected it and I am anxious to get into action.

I have several letters to write so please excuse this scribbling. Will write later after I get settled again.

---

[1]Kinnie, no record.

[2]MM2c(A) T. J. Gallivan, First Aeronautical Detachment USS *Jupiter.* Duffy, no record.

[3]NAS Dunkerque was under construction at this time and eventually became an antisubmarine U.S. Navy air patrol base on Jan. 1, 1918. It was considered the front because it was only 30 miles behind the lines and received heavy bombardment from land, sea, and air.

Will probably have something interesting to write about too.

As Ever,

Irving

Mail will reach me by this address

US Naval Aviation Forces

23 Rue De La Paix

Paris, France

Nov. 13, 1917 ❖ *Went to all the interesting places in Paris. Leaving tonight for Dunkirk.*

Nov. 14, 1917 ❖ *Arrived in Dunkirk and found the American station. Got our baggage to the Barracks and turned to on building the hangers.*

Nov. 15, 1917 ❖ *We were eating in a resturant.*

Nov. 16, 1917 ❖ *Looked at the different places that had been shelled.*

Nov. 17, 1917 ❖ *Boy told us that the Bosh* [sic] *bombed the town every other night.*

Nov. 18, 1917 ❖ *Walked around town and turned in early. Absolutely no lights in the city.*

Nov. 19, 1917 ❖ *Back to work building a dugout. Eating in our own barracks now.*

Nov. 20, 1917 ❖ *Payday drawed 325 Francs or $57.*

Nov. 21, 1917 ❖ *Had my shoes tapped. Ate supper in Dunkirk at the resturant.*

Nov. 22, 1917 ❖ *French put up a barrage* [antiaircraft] *about four o'clock in the morning and woke us all up. Thought it was another bombardment.*

Nov. 23, 1917 ✧ Got our baggage down to the station and left for Paris. Rode all night and arrived in Paris at 7 o'clock.

Nov. 24, 1917 ✧ Went to Headquarters #4 Place d'Ienna and had our picture taken for our Identification cards. Drawed 32 dollars.

Nov. 25, 1917 ✧ Went around Paris and saw a few more places such as the Opera, the St. Nazaire station.

U.S. Naval Aviation Forces
#4 Place d' Iena
Paris, France
Nov. 25, 1917

My Dear Mother,-

Just a line to let you know I have come back from the front. We had a station started up there and the Boche blew it up and now I am going to England for a while to another school where we are taught some more about aviation. It is only for a short time, just till our station gets built up again. You would laugh to see me run for a dugout when the bombs start busting around us.

The Germans dropped one right in the middle of the hangar. By the way do you know what a hangar is? It's like a big barn where we put the aeroplanes. I will write to you from England when I get there. I am at Paris now awaiting for transportation orders. How would you like to be traveling like I have been. One night you sleep in a swell hotel, the next night on a train, and the next night on the floor of an old shack. In a couple of nights more I will be bobbing up and down sleeping on the ship that takes us to Eng. It's great fun after you get used to it.

I have a whole lot to write to you but I don't know now whether half my letters gets past the censor or not. They are awfully strict about the mail. I guess I'll save it till I get back then I can tell you a bookful.

I received both packages, the one from you and the one from Laura, and spoke about them to you in my other letters.

I received a letter from Lewis the other day too. Guess I'm getting my mail from the states allright but you're not getting all of mine.

Well so long for this time.

As Ever,

Irving

Nov. 27, 1917 ✧ Went down to the YMCA with Van Golden and saw Kinney.[?]

Nov. 28, 1917 ✧ Had a good hot bath and went to a show. Left Paris at 7 A.M. and arrived in London at 12 o'clock.

Nov. 29, 1917 ✧ Proceeded to headquarters. Not a single thing to eat for 36 hours. Had such a bad cold that I could hardly speak.

Nov. 30, 1917 ✧ Landed in the Royal Naval Air Service (RNAS) at 10 o'clock at night at Cranwell, England.[4]

Dec. 1, 1917 ✧ Started to take the course in bomb dropping. Lost seabag of clothes at Le Harve, France.

---

[4]When Navy headquarters in Paris sought formal Observer training for Irving and other petty officers in the fall of 1917, they chose the British RNAS with their well-equipped aviation training centers at Cranwell and Eastchurch/Leysdown. The Royal Naval Air Station at Cranwell was located in Lincolnshire, 32 miles NNW of London and due west of "The Wash" on England's east coast, and Eastchurch/Leysdown is east of London at the mouth of the Thames River on the Isle of Sheppey. At this and other RNAS stations, all the traditions of the Royal Navy were strictly observed. When referring to taking meals, an officer of the Royal Navy would tell you, "THEY mess, WE dine!"

Dec. 2, 1917 ✧ *Very cold day. Stayed in the barracks all day and read. My cold was getting better after I had attended the sick bay for a few days.*

Dec. 3, 1917 ✧ *Machine fell and pilot was killed and burned to a crisp.*

Dec. 4, 1917 ✧ *Had a letter from Ada today. Studying bomb dropping, bomb loading and the different kinds of sights.*

Dec. 5. 1917 ✧ *Englishmen gave us a blowout. Singing, speaking and toasts were given to Wilson and king.*[5]

Dec. 6, 1917 ✧ *Big raid on London. Report that two German machines were brought down.*

Dec. 7, 1917 ✧ *Went to the R.N.A.S. concert tonight.*

Dec. 8, 1917 ✧ *Had a review on the Lewis Mch. Gun. Dropped some bombs with the equal distance sight and looked over all the machines in Hangars in the afternoon.*

Dec. 9, 1917 ✧ *Read all day. Wrote a letter to Mamma. Very foggy all day and no flying.*

U.S. Naval Aviation Forces

#4 Place d' Iena

Paris, France

Somewhere in England [Cranwell]

Dec. 9, 1917

Dear Mother,-

I wrote a letter to you while I was in Paris and I thought you might like to have one from England. We are at school and studying hard again. Seems as though they can't teach us enough.

---

[5]U.S. President Woodrow Wilson and Britain's King George V.

I like it very well here. I can talk with everybody and beside the food is fine and plenty of it.

I had it all over again to learn the different values of money. They use pounds, shillings, florins, sixpence and half pennys.

If you have say twenty dollars in you pocket, they say you have four pounds in your pocket. By Golly! I could carry a couple of ton then, and never notice it.

I had a letter from cousin Ada telling me all about the time they had out to Schoharie [N.Y.] also some pictures that she took. Laura and Lewis were in them. she said that Lewis had been to New York and they had tired him all out in one day.

She said Settone [Bower, cousin] was in training not far from Chicago. The night I stayed in New York all my aunts (except one and after a while two) didn't think very much of my undertaking. I wonder what they thought about Settone.

He is in a worse fix than I am being married and I'll bet he isn't drawing near as much money as I am and a wife to support. Well, I suppose it was my luck, that I wasn't hooked up at that. I diden't tell you that I was corresponding with a little French girl. She is about twenty years old and "pretty" is no name for her. She writes to me in French and I write to her in English. "By Gosh" but I have the darndest time to read it sometimes, that I have to have someone who knows french to help me. I guess you know how I like someone else to read my letters too. I am only doing it to learn the language a little better.

I told you in other letters that I have made an allotment of forty dollars a month to you, from which I wish you would pay my bills such as insurance, lodge, etc. The rest you can use if you need it or save it for me.

I told you that I had received the box and the package from Laura. I had a letter from Lewis a short time ago saying you had not heard about my getting them.

He said that my old friend Harold Ross had joined the Aviation forces. He sure is a fine lad and well adapted for aviation. I hope he makes a good flier.

I bought a pair of goggles so you needn't bother sending those I asked for. I used to fly without any but my eyes bothered me so after I came down that I decided to cut it out. I use the helmet and sweater all the time. I wish the helmet was four times as heavy and a little smaller though. Ada made me one which is on the way. I hope its good and heavy.

You don't tell me much about how you are getting along with things. How is Mr. Smith getting along? Does he have lots of work? I diden't know Alice was a stenographer. Why the doost do you send my letters to New York for? It would be better if you would send them to Olive, she dosen't get much mail from me, and she tells me how anxious she is to hear about me. Well, I was anxious to hear from her one time too but it diden't do me any good. Don't take me serious, especially on this last paragraph I just wrote. I still like her but I'm a little more independent about it. Well, Au Revoir,

Irving

Dec. 10, 1917 ✧ *Made a flight with an English officer in a Neuport Machine this morning.[6] Air was fine and country beautiful. Up about thirty minutes.*

---

[6]Probably the two-seat Nieuport corps-reconnaissance biplane with either a single 110 or 130 hp engine providing a maximum speed of 91 mph at a service ceiling of 13,000 ft. It carried a single, free Lewis machine gun on Scarff ring mount for the observer in the rear cockpit. These planes served on the western front until early 1917 and were replaced by the Sopwith 1½ Strutter at which time they were used for training in Great Britain. (Thetford, *Aircraft of the 1914–1918 War,* p. 76)

Dec. 11, 1917 ✧ *Studied about ammunition and high explosives today.*

Dec. 12, 1917 ✧ *Turned in our bedding and got ready to move again in the morning.*

Dec. 13, 1917 ✧ *Left RNAS Cranwell, England. at 8:30 A.M. Arrived in Eastchurch at 10 P.M.*

Dec. 14, 1917 ✧ *English had an idea we had joined the Eng. Navy and tried to make us drill their way. Nothing doing.*

Dec. 15, 1917 ✧ *Started all over again on the Lewis Gun. Had to fall in at 6:30 AM and fell out at 7:00 PM*

Dec. 16, 1917 ✧ *Took a shower bath, a shave and general cleaning up. Read a book in afternoon.*

Dec. 17 thru 22, 1917 ✧ *Had machine gun firing today. Made a flight with an English officer in a BE-2 on Friday the 14th.[7] Up about three quarters of an hour. This was to try us out on how we liked the air. Of course all of us were well used to it. Then we started our bomb dropping course. Dropped with the mirror from 500, 1000, 2000 & 3000. Then we took up 8 incendiary bombs and dropped them from the same altitudes also 4000. After we did the bombs we did the machine gun.*

---

[7] Geoffrey de Havilland's B.E.2 was a 70 hp Renault-powered, two-place reconnaissance biplane with a maximum speed of 70 mph at sea level. It began life in 1912 and was the first British aircraft to land in France at the start of the war, arriving there on August 13, 1914, and made one of the earliest reconnaissance flights behind the lines. A B.E.2C, piloted by RFC Lt. F. Sowrey of No. 39 Sqdn., is credited with bringing down the German Zeppelin L.32 before the B.E.2 was retired to training. Although a conventional, tractor-driven biplane, its two forward nose skids, a long, skinny fuselage, and an upper wing that looked like it had been mounted far too high gave it a distinctly fragile, prewar appearance, which was its true genesis. (Thetford, *Aircraft of the 1914–1918 War*, p. 3)

Dec. 23 and 24, 1917 ✧ *Saturday night we went to London and spent Sunday there at the Y.M.C.A. Were invited to a millionaire home to tea and danced with a little actress. Left on the 5:45 train at Charing Cross for Kent Co. Westerham.*[8]

Dec. 25 and 26, 1917 ✧ *Had Christmas dinner of turkey and plum pudding. My suprise to draw a piece of coin, a wedding ring and two little porcelain babies.*

Dec. 27 thru 31, 1917 ✧ *Arrived in Eastchurch on time and in the morning went to Leysdown to do our machine gun work.*[9] *Fired six pans at the target in the water. Rec'd a high mark.*[10] *Then we had a little practise on jams. Then we went up and fired at a kite. Rec'd a very good mark on it too. Had to fix a lot of jams behind propellor.*[11] *These days are very cold and flying isn't very desirable. Well, tomorrow is New Years and we have to fly again.*

Jan. 1 and 2, 1918 ✧ *Today we were up five times dropping bombs. I*

---

[8] A small photo of a British family of six is in Irving's extensive World War I photo collection. On the back is printed, "With Best Wishes from Lord and Lady Swaythling & family to their American friends. Townhill Park, Nr. Southampton."

[9] Leysdown is yet another RNAS training site also on the Isle of Sheppey two miles east of Eastchurch.

[10] The "Pan" or ammunition holder for the Lewis machine gun is a round, drum-shaped, sheet-metal housing that contains 97 rounds of .303 British ammunition. The cartridges are arranged radially in the pan in two parallel layers. The loaded pan is dropped over a post on the top of the weapon and locked into place. (*Savage-Lewis Automatic Machine Gun, Air-Cooled, Gas-Operated, Model 1915* [Utica, N.Y.: Savage Arms Co., reprint, Forest Grove, Oregon: Normount Armament Co., 1970], pp. 12, 23)

[11] Many photos from those early days, including one in Irving's collection, show a plane in the air and someone outside the cockpit, standing on the wing, reaching forward presumably to make in-flight repairs.

dropped my first live bombs, four sixteen lbs. and one a hundred and
twelve lbs. from fifteen hundred feet. Made a dead hit with it.

Jan. 3, 1918 ✧ *Today we started our Observers course and started out*
with wireless, semaphore and flashing.

Jan. 4 and 5, 1918 ✧ *Today we had navigation and I guess it is about*
the fifth time but this is going to prove the best I think.

> U.S. Naval Aviation Forces
> #4 Place d' Iena
> Paris, France
> Somewhere in England
> Jan. 4, 1918

Dear Lewis,-

Received your letter of Nov. 3 and glad to get it, altho it was
a little late for Christmas.

I am at a different station again still training and believe me I'm
getting some training too. Before long I will be probably able to
tell you something wonderful. I won't be able to mention it now
as I want to wait until I know its a sure thing. I like to have things
coming and I thought maybe you would like to have it that way
too.[12]

This last week I have been doing a lot of flying. Three to five
flights a day and averaging about four thousand feet each.

On one trip I dropped sixteen bombs (small) on another I
dropped a hundred and twelve pounder. By Gosh but that big
one sure made a jar. This is the kind we use on submarines so you
can imagine what they are like.

---

[12]Pilot officers tried but failed to obtain commissions for their observers.

I expect to go back to France in a couple of weeks and I guess its business too.

I don't like to go back to Dunkirk. Its a rotten place and the Huns bomb it every moonlight night, so you see that sometimes you don't get much sleep. Besides its not very pleasant to be standing in a dugout half dressed either.

I've had so many letters lately that I can hardly find time to answer them.

I wrote a letter to Mamma from London the day before Christmas. I didn't know exactly what or how I was going to spend the day. But being lucky I fell in on an invitation to the country to spend the Holidays. I surely had a dandy time too. There was only two of us and we stayed from Monday night (24) till Wed. the 26th. We had a big Turkey dinner, Plum pudding and a funny thing about the pudding. I found a piece of coin, a wedding ring and two porcelain babies in it. Well they had a good laugh you see. They were very nice people and also very rich so you see we spent Christmas in quite some class.

I'll bet you did suprise the people in New York. How does Aunt Carrie feel about Settone's being away. I remember how she took on when I went away, and Aunt Dora too.

Today is Sunday and this afternoon I went up and looped the loop in a tractor machine three times. I suppose you think that is quite a stunt, don't you? Well, there is absolutely no sensation to it. I'll show you how to do it in a little diagram.[13]

Flying along on the level, nose her over a little to pick up good speed and then pull back sharply on the joy stick and over you go. Clear as mud, Eh?

---

[13]Irving drew a one-line sketch that is a horizontal line, then dives down at a sharp angle, then the loop and return to level flight.

These machines make a hundred and twenty miles an hour. To get a shave just stick you head out the cockpit and you get a close one. The whiskers that don't get blown off get pushed back in, you see.

Did you get my other letters in which I spoke about my allotment and other things?

I haven't had a letter stating that you know anything about this. I think I have spoke about it three or four times.

I want to be sure that you are getting it all right. it is to the amount of forty dollars and begins with the month of November and I made it for six months. After it runs out I'll renew it and increase it if possible.

Well I think I have told you everything for this time. I will close hoping this finds you all well. I am,

As Ever,

Irving

Please excuse this writing as I haven't any pen besides nothing to write on except my lap.[14]

I have a letter from a little girl in France. She is about 20 years old and very pretty. It may amuse you to read it. Will find it enclosed.[15]

Jan. 6, 1918 ✧ *I received quite a lot of mail this week and I am going to try and answer them tomorrow.*

Jan. 7, 1918 ✧ *Made a flight today and did the loop three times.*[16] *Wrote a letter to Lewis.*

---

[14]Letter was written with a blue coloring pencil.

[15]In Irving's collection there are three French picture post-cards from a French girl. Both the pictures and the messages are quite innocent.

[16]Inferred statements of piloting can be neither proved nor disproved at this time. Irving gave his son, Roger, a pair of Navy aviator wings of 1920

Jan. 8, 1918 ✧ *On the switchboard learning W/T also the flashlight reading.*

Jan. 9, 1918 ✧ *Received a box of cigars from Uncle Frank for Christmas. Quite a lot of mail lately.*

Jan. 10, 1918 ✧ *Studied about the RNAS aviation camera, also navigation.*

Jan. 11, 1918 ✧ *Drawed nine Pounds English money = $43.80. Beginning to receive six words a minute on the wireless. Visual sig. is coming with much difficulty.*

Jan. 12, 1918 ✧ *Flying today with Visual Lamp. Found it rather a hard proposition.*[17]

Jan. 13, 1918 ✧ *Wrote letters all afternoon and sent a photo to Miss Estelle.*[18]

Jan. 14, 1918 ✧ *Wrote letters today too. Some of the boys went to Chatham and Sheerness.*[19] *They bought crab medicine, itch medicine for all of us had the French itch.*

---

design without explanation. Irving's name is not among the list of enlisted pilots.

[17]Visual Lamp signaling with Morse Code is probably difficult to send or receive while one is being tossed around in bumpy air.

[18]Irving was long overdue in answering a picture postcard from M'Estelle dated Oct. 30, 1917. It is addressed to: School of Aviation, Cazaux, Girond [after a red line through Moutchic] "Dear Friend, I am very surprised not to receive word from you. Could you be ill? Could you have changed countries? I think that you must have received my last card Thanking you for yours. When you write to me put: M'Estelle 1 Rue Jules Barbier, St. Raphael . . . Accept, My Dear Friend, my warm Friendship. M'Estelle."

[19]Chatham and Sheerness are both on the Isle of Sheppey.

Jan. 15, 1918 ✧ *Had spotting today and Navigation also.*

Jan. 16, 1918 ✧ *Wireless and ship spotting. Rained all day and the mud is over three inches deep.*

Jan. 17, 1918 ✧ *Took out $10,000 insurance policy today payable to Mamma. If I should be killed she would receive $57 a month for 240 months.*

Jan. 18, 1918 ✧ *Also made out another allotment. I was to send $15 and the government would send $10 makin $25 all told.*[20]

Jan. 19, 1918 ✧ *Rec'd package of candy from Mr. Shrieves also five letters.*

Jan. 20, 1918 ✧ *Flying this afternoon reconnaissance #2 over Sheerness reporting all shipping in the harbor.*[21]

Jan. 21, 1918 ✧ *Flew in the Neuport and did Hygthe gun camera work.*[22]

---

[20] "Although benefits of various kinds date back to colonial days, veterans of WWI were the first to receive disability compensation, allotments for dependents, life insurance, medical care, and vocational rehabilitation." (*Information Please Almanac* [Boston: Houghton Mifflin, 1989], p. 309)

[21] RNAS squadrons were identified with a single digit such as "Naval 2." After incorporation along with the RFC into the RAF on April 1, 1918, all former RNAS squadrons had 200 added to their existing numbers. Thus Naval 2 became RAF 202 Squadron. Irving would later fly over the lines in Europe with this same 202 reconnaissance squadron.

[22] Mr. Stewart K. Taylor, London, Ontario, Canada, renowned British/Canadian military historian, generously furnished the following in a letter of April 7, 1992: "The *Hythe* camera gun was a regulation Lewis machine gun (minus the top pan of ammunition), modified to accommodate single frame photography. With each pull of the trigger a single frame was exposed. The Hythe camera gun was mounted on the observer's gun mounting in the rear cockpit of the Nieuport two-seater. A concentric ringed bullseye on the camera overlapped that portion of the aircraft he shot at. This device was successfully used in simulated air-to-air combat at Hythe, England, where

Jan. 22, 1918 ✧ *Observer work going on just the same. W/T coming fine.*

Jan. 23 and 24, 1918 ✧ *Van Golden machine run out of gas while over the water and he managed to plane down to land but got smashed up a bit. Broke his new glasses. Very lucky to get out as easy as that.*

Jan. 25, 1918 ✧ *Went to moving pictures in L Shed. They were quite amusing.*

Jan. 26, 1918 ✧ *Boys went to London and I stayed in camp.*

Jan. 27, 1918 ✧ *Wrote letters all day Sunday. Also washed some clothes. Had very good eating today. 14 mens rations.*

Jan. 28, 1918 ✧ *Flew in Newport on exercise of Hythe gun camera. Was up forty min. with F.S.L. Lawson.*

Jan. 29, 1918 ✧ *Flew for #4 reconnaissance over Leysdown to draw map of trenches.*[23]

Jan. 30, 1918 ✧ *F.S.L. Fowler looped twice and came down three thousand feet in a nose spin, a few stalls and side slips. Raid tonight.*

Jan. 31, 1918 ✧ *Went up to do photography in Farman but motor was bad so diden't do any.*[24] *Raid tonight.*

---

the modification was first made, and gave the person using it a print of just how close his marksmanship was."

[23]Leysdown, on the Isle of Sheppey, is one of the direct approaches to London, when flying from Germany. Again, Mr. Stewart K. Taylor included the following helpful information in his letter of April 7, 1992: "There was at least one battery of guns mounted at Leysdown. Trenches were dug into the coastal landscape, originally for home defense but they served more as a propaganda deterrent than anything else. The most useful service of the trenches was to provide the novice RNAS pilots and observers with an example of Western Front style trenches from which they could better their knowledge of photographic and visual aerial reconnaissance."

[24]See Chapter 3 (Sept. 3, 1917, footnote 3) for Farman aircraft data.

Feb. 1, 1918 ❖ *Made first hop on W/T in a Curtiss.*[25]

Feb. 2, 1918 ❖ *My first hop on spotting. Still working on W/T getting about 10 words a minute.*

Feb. 3, 1918 ❖ *Made a flight with W/T and could receive very good. Rained today.*

US Naval Aviation Forces
#4 Place d' Iena
Paris, France
Feb. 3, 1918

Dear Lewis,-

I have three letters which I have received within the past week. Part of the last one is from Mamma. I am going to try and answer them all together. It will save me time and besides I have a raft of others to answer.

I guess every Jane I ever knew has written to me and wants me to answer. Of course I have to be polite and do so. People I have met on the T.U. job have written to me. Those in New York, the fellows in the Hardware, some of my old school mates, my friends who have recently arrived in France, Settone for instance and Harold Ross. People at our church, and the mission. Some people I have met in France and now in England. Some strangers from out west who have seen my name in a paper and have offered to send me something. This I think was written by one of the fellows and he signed our names to it. You will see by the way they spelled my name that I had nothing to do about it. I will enclose the clipping. I think I received about six answers to it.

---

[25]Eastchurch is on the water so possibly a Curtiss HS-1 or HS-2 flying boat.

All together I think I have had about a hundred different people that have written to me.

I have made a list which I check off as I write and as I receive.

There is so many things to answer in your letters that I will go over them in pieces and do the best I can.

I am glad you found out how to clean that rifle as I was afraid it would rust on the inside. You probably understand that the barrel of a gun sweats and by some form of osmosis it gets moisture on the inside. A rag with clean oil should be run through about once a month to overcome this.

You spoke about the tools down cellar. I don't know what to say for you to do. Just use your own judgement. I think that if you take the best ones and bring them upstairs it would be a good idea.

I am glad Mamma has received the first check. I think there will be about three of them of forty then it will change to twenty five as in January we made out a new allotment of fifteen dollars and the Government adds ten to it. This I suppose is to induce every soldier and sailor in Foreign Service to send his money home which keeps some of the money in America. You see there is a great deal of it paid over here and spent here. I took out a ten thousand dollar insurance payable to Mamma at the rate of 57 dollars a month for two hundred and forty months. It cost me about six dollars and sixty six cents a month for it. It took effect I think about the 18th of Jan. 1918. The policy will be sent home to her. So let me know about all these things that they are received allright.

I am glad to hear that Frank was so successful in not getting into the service. He is too young besides there is lots of time yet. I received six cans of eats from Mr. Shrieves. I haven't wrote to him yet but will do so at the earliest opportunity. I wrote to Mr. Clapham and Mr. Simon today.

I haven't received the packages from Andy yet. By the way, what is Aunt Annie's address in Schenectady and what is her last name? I've forgotten it. Aunt Jennie told me to be sure and drop her a line when I received the box of cigars she put in with their box for me. She said she came all the way from Schenectady to bring it.

Has she been down to our place yet?

I have received two packages from cousin Ada. Some candy and a helmet some bed socks and a pair of wristlets. Guess I got enough of them things (Helmet and wristlets) now. One of my new friends in Chicago is sending me another set. I'll have to tell you something about these helmets. The first time I used the one Laura sent me, in the air here in England I nearly froze. So when I went to London I bought a leather one lined with fur. It cost me three pounds. Thats about fifteen dollars but its worth it.

You see I haven't much hair any more and of course I get cold quicker. However, I make use of it at night and use it on my head the same as I use the bed socks. You would laugh to see us when we are all ready for bed. All of us have a little patent all our own.

Last week we had two air raids and quite a number of people in London were killed over two hundred I think. We all go outside and watch the anti-aircraft guns fire away. They fly over at an altitude of twenty thousand feet and are impossible to see them even with the strong searchlight. But you can hear the peculiar roar of their motors as they pass over. The Mercedes, a German motor, has a noise that is different from any other motor.

I won't forget the first time I heard it. I was looking up trying to see the big German Gotha plane which I could hear distinctly.[26] The anti-aircraft guns were firing and the shells were

---

[26]The German Gotha G.V bomber with two Mercedes D-IVa, 260 hp engines could bomb from an operating ceiling of 21,325 ft. due, not to

bursting away up in the sky. All of a sudden I heard a piece of scrapnel [sic] coming. It was faint at first but in a second it had hit and bounded Zing and on it went with a long whining wailing sound.

I just made tracks for a dugout for they were beginning to sing all around.

However, I am well aware its high time to git under cover when the guns begin to crack close by.[27]

I am flying every day making five and six flights a day now. I think I told you something about looping in my last letter. Well the other day the air was not very bumpy and I was flying at about seven thousand ft. I looped twice and then went into a sharp spiral down for about five thousand feet. I suddenly became aware that my ears were hurting frightfully. When I landed they told me that it was due to the quick change in air pressure in coming down from a high altitude so quickly.

Well, I think we will be back in France by the first of next

---

superchargers, which had yet to be invented, but to its oversized cylinders and above-normal compression ratio. Anyone who has ever heard these slow turning (1400 RPM), inline, 6-cylinder engines operating says that the Mercedes has a sound unlike any other internal combustion engine. The 500-mile range of the Gotha was sufficient to begin daylight raids on London during June 1917, inflicting much more damage than the Zeppelins had up to that date. It was sufficient that fighter squadrons had to be brought back from France to defend against them. The Germans then turned to night raids by these giants, and these continued through May 1918. (W. M. Lamberton, comp., *Reconnaissance and Bomber Aircraft of the 1914–1918 War,* edited by E. F. Cheesman [Letchworth, England: Harleyford Publ., 1962], p. 148; Kenneth Munson, *Bombers, Patrol and Reconnaissance Aircraft, 1914–1919* [London: Blandford Press, Macmillan Co., Cassell PLC, 1968], p. 105; Herschel Smith, *Aircraft Piston Engines* [New York: McGraw-Hill, 1981], p. 36)

[27]The Isle of Sheppey, being east of London, is ideally located for antiaircraft batteries to defend the London approaches.

month. I will be glad too for I think I like France better than I do England, the climate is more agreeable to me.

Young Lasher [Herbert] is over in France. He was with me quite a while [at Moutchic]. That young fellow who you asked about has died a long time ago. He went crazy you know. Quite a few of the first lot that came over with me have been killed while in training. Their pictures were in the Leslies [British?] magazine. I saw them in it a short time ago.

I forgot to tell you I received a box of cigars from Uncle Frank. I thought it was rather nice of them to remember me.

Well I think I have told you all for this time hoping this finds you all well as I am feeling fine. I am,

As Ever,
Irving

Feb. 4, 1918 ✧ *Developed some plates and a roll of film and slept in Sunday morning.*

Feb. 5, 1918 ✧ *W/T again and gettin about 12 words today.*

Feb. 6, 1918 ✧ *Had a little test in Visual signalling and got 54% in it.*

Feb. 7, 1918 ✧ *Payday drawed $92.46. Brown [Randall R.] drawed about the same. My allotment couldn't have been taken out.*

Feb. 8, 1918 ✧ *Flying again and making W/T tests.*

U.S. Naval Aviation Forces
4 Place d' Iena
Paris, France
Feb. 18, 1918
Somewhere in England [Sheerness]

Dear Adah

I had almost given up hopes of your package ever reaching me. But at last it has reached the end of its long journey. They say good things come slow and I assure you this was more than good. The chocolate was fine. The best I've had in just one year. The other candy was tra bien too. I am saving the malted milk for the long flights out to sea where there is danger of being detained sometimes should the motor become disabled and we are forced to land. The helmet fits fine and is just what I wanted. The wristlets are dandy.

Well my time in England is getting very short. In fact I hope to be in Paris by the 19th or 20th and from there we proceed to the front.

I have done a great deal of flying while over here and have passed in everything. I feel quite confident in myself to tackle a Hun in the air.

I had a letter from Settone telling me that he was on the same side of the Big Pond as I was. Gosh! But I hope I can see him. Maybe if I am lucky I will be able to meet him in Paris when I get back. He is one of the fellows I'd like to take up in an aeroplane and scare the pudding out of. Wouldn't that be great? I suppose you think I have a peculiar liking to tease somebody. Well its not so bad to loop in an aeroplane as one would think. Its the thinking that there is nothing under you that makes you feel so funny.

Well I must close thanking you a thousand times for the two lovely packages you have sent to me.

Hoping I may hear from you again soon, I am,
As Ever,
Your cousin Irving

Feb. 21, 1918 ✧ *Getting our passing out test in W/T sending.*

Feb. 22, 1918 ✧ *Payday drawed $9.73.*

[Final entry in Irving's diary]

On Active Service with
American Expeditionary Force
Feb. 23, 1918
US Naval Aviation Forces
#4 Place d' Iena
Paris, France
Somewhere in London Tonight

Dear Momma,-

After a long stay in England I am at last on my way back to dear old France.

I am quite anxious too as I am getting rather <u>fed up</u> with this place. Notice the underline.

It is an English expression of being tired of a place.

I am wondering if you have received the last letter I wrote telling about the change in my allotment and the insurance I took out payable to you. I am not going to state particulars in this letter until I hear from you again.[28] I have finished training and have qualified in everything and passing with very high marks.

---

[28]Irving appears certain that, having completed his training, he will soon be in combat. He was very conscious of the possibilities and made sure his mother would be cared for to the best of his ability in the event of his death.

However, this high mark stuff is for my own benefit as well as the credit for it.

You see when I get in a scrap with a Hun at a height of twenty thousand feet the more capable I am why the better chance I have of staying up there and making him take the tumble.[29]

You ought to see me strutting around with a *pin,* an emblem of being qualified in the air.

Its quite neat too. It looks something like this made of silver and gold plated.

Guess I better stop telling you all this as you might think I am trying to stuff you.

I wrote a letter to Martha a couple of weeks ago.

What do you think, Settone is over in France now. I had a letter from him. He didn't say what part of France he was in.

His job is a cinch and quite safe too. He will never see any fighting as his work is in an office as I understand him.

I wouldn't trade with him on a bet. What do you think?

I haven't received the packages from Andy yet. I received the ones from cousin Ada allright.

I wrote a long letter to Lewis only a couple of weeks ago so will make this a short one.

Have just come in from seeing a free show at one of the theatres. I mean free to all in uniform.

---

[29]This statement could have been made by one just graduating from pilot training, but it is obvious that he is referring to his ability to defend himself, his pilot, and their aircraft from his place in the observer's rear cockpit with the Lewis machine gun.

I am going to bed as soon as I mail this.

Hoping this finds you well and getting along allright.

I am,

As Ever,

Irving

{ *Upon completion of the observer course, Irving and the others were awarded RNAS wings #GB-N-4. They are one-piece gilt metal construction, measuring 54mm horizontally and 12mm vertically just as Irving sketched them and very beautiful. On April 1, 1918, the RNAS and the RFC combined into one air service known to this day as the Royal Air Force (RAF), and these wings eventually were no longer issued. (D. Chalif,* Military Pilot and Aircrew Badges of the World, 1870 to Present, *Vol. I,* Europe [Albania–Hungary] *[San Jose, Calif.: Roger J. Bender Publishing Co., 1982]; R. J. Huff,* Wings and Things of the World, *No. 13 [Fall 1990], p. 36)*

This well-deserved award was soon to be taken away from these Americans because there was, at that time, no rating in the U.S. Navy for Aerial Observer. Note the following two Navy directives.}

N33-SBF-SA

24 December 1919

From: Bureau of Navigation,

To: Commanding Officer, Key West, Florida

Subject: Special device for mechanics and observers holding flight orders.

1. Despite articles in unofficial publications to the effect that a special device to be worn by mechanics and observers having flight orders has been approved, you are advised that the Bureau of Navigation has taken no action in the approval of such device.

2.You will be informed at such time as this matter may be duly authorized.

> S. Fry
> By direction

NAVY DEPARTMENT N10-G-C-5537-3732

First Endorsement   BUREAU OF NAVIGATION 6 April 1921
From: Bureau of Navigation
To: U.S. Naval Air Station, Pearl Harbor, T.H.
Subject: Aviation Insignia - half wing worn by enlisted men.
1. There is no authority for wearing a half wing aviator's device.

> Signed,
> Thomas Washington

["On March 27, 1922, to comply with a provision of the law that established the Bureau of Aeronautics, its Chief and at least 70% of its officers be either pilots or observers, the Bureau of Aeronautics defined the functions and qualifications of Naval Aviation Observers and recommended a course of study for their training. Upon its approval by the Bureau of Navigation, RADM W. A. Moffett reported for training and on 17 June 1922, qualified as the first Naval Aviation Observer." ("United States Naval Aviation 1910–1970," p. 49)]

[Ensign Curtis Seaman Read, Naval Aviator #83 and member of the First Yale Unit, arrived at NAS Dunkerque February 24, 1918, along with Petty Officer Eichelberger. These two had flown together regularly since training days at NAS Moutchic. Irving, although not at the station at this time, also knew Eichelberger. Read held "Eich" in high regard even though he was a bit brash and characterized him in a letter home, "How much kindness and real human nature there is hidden under an artificial toughness."

On February 26, 1918, Ens. Read went up for his first practice flight in a Donnet-Denhaut flying boat with its 200 hp Hisso, which appeared to be in good condition. Eichelberger was aboard sitting in the observer's forward cockpit. The seaplane escaped the hazards in and around the Dunkerque harbor and lifted off safely. The station commander, Lt. Artemus "Di" Gates, watched it turn and circle while Read familiarized himself with the controls and the tricks of handling it to the best advantage. He was apparently having no trouble.

Twenty minutes after the seaplane went up, it went into a vertical nose-dive, fell like a stone, and crashed into the water. A launch reached the spot in a few minutes.

Read was found, still alive in the wreckage of the plane, but he soon expired. The body of Petty Officer Eichelberger was not found. It finally washed ashore at La Panne on July 8th. The Donnet-Denhaut flying boat with its erratic Hisso was an unforgiving French partner to an inexperienced aviator such as Read.

(Ralph D. Paine, The First Yale Unit, *Vol. I–II [New York: Riverside Press, 1925], Vol. II, p. 195; Log of U.S. NAS Dunkerque, France, spring 1918, National Archives, Washington, D.C.; Herbert Lasher, Letter(s) written to L. Sheely)]*

On Active Service with the
American Expeditionary Forces
Mar. 2, 1918
US Naval Aviation Forces
#4 Place d' Iena
Paris, France

Dear Mamma,-

I promised to write a letter when I got back to France. Well here I am in Paris perfectly well and in good spirits.

I have eased my appetite which I was unable to do in England. You see on account of the food shortage there.

Since I've come back to France the second time it seems Oh so much better. Just like a place I've known all my life.

We were in England during the poorest season and at times it was rather disagreeable.

I have been out walking today and tonight. I am going to get a good sleep.

On our journey across the channel which included three nights I have had very little sleep. The little I did get was in such bad conditions that it didn't do me much good.

I don't know what to write sometimes as we are limited to what we can say.

I would like to tell you where we are going and what we are going to do but I think you will have to guess them.

I hope you understand all I've told you about concerning the insurance.

How is everything at home?

Have you received all the letters I sent to you from England?

It is almost a year since I enlisted. Does it seem as long as that to you?

I have had a great deal of experience in one year too. Guess I know quite a lot about this Old World of ours now.

Well, I think this is all for this time hoping this finds all of you well, I am

As Ever,
Irving

CHAPTER 5

Dunkerque NAS, the RAF, and Clermont-Ferrand

March 3 to June 26, 1918

[*Early 1918 was marked in eastern Europe by the withdrawal from the war of two of the Allied nations. On March 3, Russia signed the Treaty of Brest-Litovsk, which put an end to the war between that nation and the Central Powers. On May 7, Rumania also made peace with the Central Powers when leaders signed the Treaty of Bucharest.*]

> US Naval Aviation
> #4 Place d' Iena
> Paris, France
> Mar. 17, 1918

Dear Mamma,-

I have three letters and one post card from home. They include a note from Frank, Mr. Smith, you and Lewis.

The card is dated Jan. 23 and the letters Dec. 10, Jan. 25 and Feb. 3. I think I am receiving all your letters. The only trouble is with the packages. They are very slow in coming across. I have not received the Fountain Pen from the Tabernacle or the ones from Andy or the ones from Scott Walrath. They will probably turn up in the future if they are not lost.

I am wondering how fast he can receive radio by now. At the end of two months with a practice of about a half an hour a day I could receive fourteen words of a four letter group or fifty six letters a minute.[1]

So he enjoyed the letter from my Francais girl. I write to her just for curiosity besides it helps me to learn French.[1]

I was very much pleased with Frank's and Mr. Smith's letters. I like to read what they have to say in their own way of writing it.

Although I am not answering them separately and directly I know that they read all the letters that I write home.

I am glad you are receiving the allotment allright. Did you get the letter telling about the insurance policy I took out. It is for ten-thousand dollars. It costs me about six-dollars and sixty cents a month.[2]

The benefactor [beneficiary] is paid fifty seven dollars a month for twenty years in case of death. It also insures in case of accident and all in all is a very good thing.

After six payments on my other allotment there will probably be a change for I made out another in which I think I have to pay fifteen dollars and the government pays or adds ten to it making twenty five all told. I made this out while in England and haven't heard anything more about it.

At the time they told me that my other allotment would be stopped immediately and this new one go in effect.

Well, I think I will tell you something about what I am doing. We left "*Old Blighty*" as the English call it (England) and went to Paris. It wasn't a "bon voyage" however, but we were glad to get back to France.

---

[1]"He" referred to twice in this letter is an unknown, possibly his brother Lewis.

[2]World War II servicemen also had access to $10,000 Life Insurance for $6.60 per month.

I was suprised at how I had forgotten the language. I was in Paris three days, had lots of good things to eat which I couldn't buy in England and then left for our station the same one you mentioned [NAS Dunkerque].

I haven't done very much flying as yet, only three or four hops so far. You see we have only been here a little over a week.

Our grub is fine too. We appreciate it so much better after being in England where they nearly starved us.

I was suprised at one of the fellows telling me when I came back that I was looking fat. However I realize that I hadn't done a whole lot of manual labor on the other hand it was mostly brain work. This is the only reason I can give for being fat.

In fact I only weigh about fourteen stone [196 lbs] and am worth about thirty pounds.

I also drank tea four times a day.

There is a young lad from Albany who is with me and he gets the Knickerbocker Press and he lets me read them all.[3]

So you see I get quite a lot of news.

I have so many letters to write and our letters are limited to what we put in them that I find it quite a difficult proposition to sit down and write.

You pass the letters around to so many different ones that it queers me from making duplicate copies.

Well, I think this will be all for this time, hoping this finds you well, I am,

As Ever,
Irving

[*On April 1, 1918, while he was at USNAS Dunkerque, Irving's rating was advanced from MM2C/A to MM1C/A (Machinist Mate*

---

[3]A second Albany, N.Y. newspaper.

Aviation Petty Officer First Class Irving E. Sheely, newly arrived back in France, proudly wears his Aerial Observer wings after completing the Royal Naval Air Service course in England. (Courtesy of Roger Sheely)

First Class / Air). (Irving E. Sheely, U.S. Navy Service Record from March 28, 1917, to August 22, 1922)
    He has now been in the Navy one year with 10 months of that time overseas duty.]

[*On April 1, 1918, the Royal Flying Corps (RFC) and the Royal Naval Air Service (RNAS) were combined to form a single service known to this day as the Royal Air Force (RAF).*

Within the RAF was the 5th Group, 61st Wing located at Bergues, six miles southeast of Dunkerque. The 61st Wing consisted of three squadrons:
    202 Squadron—Reconnaissance, operating two place DH-4 aircraft
    213 Squadron—Fighters, operating single place Camel aircraft
    217 Squadron—Bombing (antisubmarine) operating two place DH-4 aircraft
    Upon completion of the RNAS Aerial Observer course, Irving was sent back to NAS Dunkerque and from there temporarily assigned to 202 Squadron, RAF (formerly Naval #2), for his first air combat mission. After one patrol over the lines, he was recalled to NAS Dunkerque. There they resumed over-water, antisubmarine patrols in the French Donnet-Denhaut flying boats.
    (G. E. Sprague, "Flying Gobs," Liberty Magazine, Jan. 7, 14, 21, 1939. In this article, George Sprague, member First Aeronautic Detachment, relates an account of his service as a DH-4 bomber pilot with RAF 217 Squadron.)]

[*Despite the victories over Russia and Rumania, the Germans now knew that submarine warfare alone would not take Great Britain out of the war. On March 21 Germany launched an all-out assault, expecting to force a decision before American troops could take up positions in force. The opening drive was directed at the British front south of Arras with Paris as the objective. Although it successfully pushed the lines back forty miles, it was finally halted on April 5. During April a second German thrust took Messines Ridge and Armentieres from the British.*]

U.S. Naval Aviation Forces
#4 Place d' Iena
Paris, France
April 10, 1918
"Somewhere in France" [Bergues]

Dear Laura and Alice,-

Received your letter the other day and as today is foggy there isn't any flying for us so I am going to write letters. I generally write the first one home and leave the rest till after. Your letter contained a lot of interesting news. It makes me think that there is still a place called home and that it is still going in the same old regime.

I have been transferred to an English Squadron temporarily.

My work is therefore somewhat different. All of it being done at an altitude of twenty thousand feet and over. Working at this extreme height has many difficulties. Intense cold, thin air and many other things. However, they supply us with electric heated suits and oxygen to overcome them. As yet I haven't been over the lines but hope to sometime this week if the weather permits. Then I will be able to tell you more about it. Possibly I will have a chance to tell you about my first encounter with the Boche.

If a year ago had somebody told me that I would be flying over Germany I would have considered them rather unbalanced. But today I think of it as the little incidents of a daily routine. I have had so many experiences, uncommon in civil life, that they are beginning to be less thrilling. I absolutely never think of danger which perhaps has something to do with it.

Mamma has been saying that she was looking in the Journal for something. Tell her to keep looking as that was what I was referring to sometime ago. Of course good things come slow and possibly it will take a little time but I'm quite sure its on the way.[4]

The first of April I was rated first class increasing my pay to, I think, ninety nine a month. I haven't drew any since being rated, so I am not sure exactly what it is. Anyway its climbing and which of course pleases me to think I am doing some good. I had a letter from Scottie saying that he has sent another package but up to date I have not received any of the ones you told me about. There is a fountain pen from the Tabernacle, two packages from Andy, two from Scottie that I remember of that are still missing. I hope they will turn up in the future. Oh! by the way, two weeks ago I received the box from the people I told you about in Chicago that had written to me. They sent it sometime in November and it reached here the last of March. There were a lot of nice things in it. One of those sleeveless sweaters and wristlets. I think I have about four pair of those wristlets now and not used one yet. It also contained three pair of socks, a full carton of Bull-Durham tobacco,[5] a dozen packs of Fatima [Turkish] cigarettes,

---

[4]Apparently his officers continue to tell him that they can obtain an officer's commission for him and some of the other qualified aerial observers.

[5]Bull-Durham tobacco was sold in small, cloth bags with a drawstring closure at the top. When kept in a shirt pocket, the string, with its handy Bull-Durham disc, was left hanging out like a watch fob. There were many variations to the procedure, but basically, to create a do-it-yourself cigarette, a single tissue of paper, kept for this purpose, is removed from a folder and held in the left hand in the form of a "U." The right hand opens the top of the tobacco bag by pulling one side while the other side is held by the teeth. The right hand then pours a small amount of tobacco into the curled paper. One of the two drawstrings at the top of the bag is again held in the teeth, and the right hand pulls the second drawstring, closing the top; the bag is returned to a shirt pocket. With two hands now available, the tongue moistens the lengthwise, glued edge of the paper, and the tobacco and paper are rolled into the familiar tube. However, because the tobacco is loose, the ends have to be twisted closed to prevent the tobacco from falling out. One

some chocolate bars, raisins, candy, gum and mints. On top of all this I received a letter from her the other day saying that she was sending me another box of nice things. Apparently she is very well to do, in fact the boys here from Chicago say that the address is in millionaire row. But she is married and has a daughter fifteen years old "*So don't worry*". Guess I'll keep till I get back anyway.

Well I think I have told you all the news I can think of now. I am in the best of health and pink of condition, am getting good substantial food which is all I can wish for.

Guess I'll have to tell you about my hair. Well there is a few straggling ones on top which I shave off to make them come in stronger or perhaps save them from falling out too. Possibly that old saying is true, "One can't have brains and hair too."

Well, I must close hoping this finds you all well, I am, as ever,

Irving

[*On December 28, 1917, British Vice-Admiral Sir Roger Keyes was placed in charge of the Dover Patrol. Since 1915 the Dover Patrol had been trying with mines and nets to inhibit the flow of German submarines moving through the English channel to the Atlantic Ocean. Keyes tried improvements to that scheme but with only marginal success. Being a man of action, he envisaged a more ambitious scheme.*

The submarines were operating out of German-occupied Belgium.

---

hand reaches in a trouser pocket for a long, wooden match. The thumbnail or pant leg ignites the match. The cigarette is lit. After a few puffs, it is down to the last shreds of tobacco in less time than it took to create it. The hand/ eye coordination necessary to roll-your-own was equivalent to that necessary in some of today's computer games, and Uncle Irving could roll a cigarette outdoors in a moderate wind, all the while maintaining a running conversation.

Specifically, they were based at Bruges, eight miles inland from the North Sea. A canal leads straight from Bruges to the North Sea at Zeebrugge. A second, smaller and longer canal from Bruges also led to the sea in an arc, terminating at the port city of Ostende.

It was Keyes' plan to sail old nineteenth-century cruisers into the canal mouth at both port cities and scuttle them, preventing the use of Bruges as a resupply base.

A heavily fortified, curving mole extended out from the shore at Zeebrugge, which first had to be engaged by a seaborne assault to allow the blockships to enter the canal mouth and scuttle themselves. To accomplish this plan, a large naval and marine amphibious force was assembled on the coast of England.

The first attempt was on the night of April 11, 1918, but was recalled before it was detected by the Germans. The wind had changed direction and would have prevented a planned ship-laid smoke screen from being effective.

A second attempt was made on the night of April 12, 1918, but it too was abandoned because of the weather. At 0001 hours on April 23, 1918, the British Cruiser Vindictive *closed with the sea side of the Zeebrugge mole after receiving intense fire from German batteries and discharged a force of Royal Marines and sailors. At the same time the cruisers* Thetis, Iphigenia, *and* Intrepid *made their way around the mole to the canal entrance.* Thetis *ran aground outside the canal, but* Iphigenia *and* Intrepid *were scuttled successfully at the canal entrance. The position of these two scuttled ships only partially blocked the canal entrance. A submarine could, with care, be warped around these vessels.*

Ostende was also attacked that night, but unsuccessfully. Later tries had only a measure of success. Therefore, facilities at Bruges continued operational, and further aerial bombardment was necessary after that date.

(James W. Stock, Zeebrugge—23 April 1918 *[Battle Book #31] [New York: Ballantine Books, Random House, 1974])*

U.S. Naval Air Station
Dunkerque, France
April 29, 1918

My Dear Mother,-

I received your most welcome letter a few days ago and this is the first opportunity I've had to write any letters.

I have been working late every day this week getting my machine in flying condition. I suppose you wonder at this but you see I have to fly in it and I want to be sure that all the wires and struts are exactly right and that the engine is running properly for myself.

I had a letter from Laura and Lewis also, so I'll make this one answer them all. Laura is doing fine on the typewriter and I'm glad to hear about Alice doing so well. Frank and Lewis are getting along great in their work too.

Well, I will tell you a little of what I've been doing. A little over a week ago [April 12, 1918] I made my first flight over the enemy territory.[6]

Two machines were scheduled to leave the aerodrome at five o'clock sharp [p.m.] and I was to go in one of them.

---

[6]Irving had been temporarily assigned to RAF 202 Reconnaissance Squadron based at Berques SE of Dunkerque:

RAF SQUADRON RECORD BOOK

Date: 12 April 1918	Duty: W/T Fleet Patrol & Coastal Reconn.		No. 202 Squadron	
			Hour of:	
Type & No.	Pilot	Observer	Start	Return
DH-4 N5962	Lt. Coulthard,	P.O. Sheely	1715	1935
Remarks:		U.S.N.		

Attacked by 10 E.A. [enemy aircraft] off Ostende at 1900 hrs. Pilot fired about 69 rounds and Observer fired about 130 rounds. E.A. used explosive bullets, machine being hit. Height 17000 ft. Visibility fair.

Naval Aviation Petty Officers all suited up for a flight: on the left, Irving E. Sheely, and on the right, probably his friend Randall R. Browne (Courtesy of Roger Sheely)

We climbed to an altitude of 18,000 feet and proceeded on to our objective. We were unmolested however until on our way home after nearly two hours flying when I noticed far, far below me (over three miles) the flashing of guns and I was well aware that the anti-aircraft guns were firing at us. Suddenly the shells were bursting all around me. We altered our course a little but still they seemed to break terribly close. Presently they stopped and out of the sky came a machine. He was a type of aeroplane I was unfamiliar with and I couldn't see his colors. As he closed in I caught a glance of the iron cross and I knew too well that the time I had been waiting for had come. At the same moment I also saw that there were more of them and they were all around me, above and below.

I had not long to wait for pop! pop! pop! and he was firing at me. My machinegun shoots at the rate of six hundred rounds a minute and I turned and opened fire.

For the first time in my life I realized that I was aiming to kill a man. I made it so warm for him that he didn't stick. But this wasn't all, the other machines opened up and the bullets were whizzing all around me. Thus we fought, dived and climbed for advantageable positions. Evidently they were intent on getting us, for they pressed the battle hard.

During the thickest of it I observed one of the Huns to dive. Down, down he went for about ten thousand feet and then he tumbled.

I could not watch him further for there was two more of the others and one was firing at me again.

We fought for over twenty minutes and presently they all drew away for we were getting over our own ground again.[7]

---

[7]This two-plane reconnaissance flight of 202 Squadron was attacked by either German Marine Jagdstaffel 1 or 2 because both squadrons of D.5

In a long steep dive from that height it took us only a short time to get home and we landed on the aerodrome at just seven thirty. The sun was just passing below the horizon. It had been a beautiful day and I was just simply thrilled with my first experience.

Immediately upon landing we inspected our machines and found twenty bullet holes and two scrapnel [sic] holes in the two machines. One of the bullets passing within three inches of my hide. I judged it was a very good miss and a little patch would fix the fabric.

However, I know that there were several Hun machines that needed patching too, except one who is beyond patching. We were very much pleased to think that we were able to hold our own, of two machines, against ten Huns.

Well, I'm quite a hero around camp now as I am the first American flier in the U.S. Naval Air Service to go over the lines and have a scrap.[8]

The boys call me "The Hun Getter" and all such foolish names.

Albatros scouts operated over that particular sector during April 1918. The single-seat Albatros fighter was an early but unsuccessful attempt at streamlined aircraft design. It never did well against the boxy British DH-4 bomber and had a bad history of shedding its wings in a steep dive. It was powered by the ever-popular 180 hp Mercedes inline 6. (Letter from British/Canadian military historian, Mr. Stewart K. Taylor, London, Ontario, Canada, dated Nov. 23, 1987; W. M. Lamberton, comp., *Reconnaissance and Bomber Aircraft of the 1914–1918 War,* edited by E. F. Cheesman [Letchworth, England: Harleyford Publ., 1960])

[8]This statement requires some qualification. No doubt he was the first Navy enlisted observer to fly over the lines and engage the Germans in air combat, but Navy Lts. Ingalls and MacLeish had already been in air combat over the lines as pilots with RAF 213 Squadron.

Even though Petty Officer Irving E. Sheely is completely covered, his face was frozen on one of the high-altitude aerial missions over the lines. (Courtesy of Roger Sheely)

Well, it was so cold up there that although I was dressed in furs and my face completely covered excepting a place to breathe, I froze my nose and lips and both cheeks so bad that they all turned brown and peeled off. I am very nearly healed up already. However, it has been very tender to shave and I have grown a tre-jolle mustache to prevent irritating my lip which was the worst place frozen.

We have other things that keep us informed that the war is still on. We are so close to the lines that the guns sound like the constant roar of thunder. Nearly every day and sometimes at night a gun fires a sixteen inch shell at us. One of these broke within forty yards of me a short time ago. Well, it jarred me up a bit. I was lying on my bunk at the time and a piece of the shell came through the roof and hit on the foot of my bunk.

Well, all the rest dusted for the dugout and I thought it wasn't a bad idea for me to do the same thing. They were dropping every seven minutes and it was no telling where the next one was going to hit.

Besides all this they come over in droves loaded with bombs. The place is so riddled that it is hardly possible to go any-where without passing a place where a bomb has not dropped. ... [9] ... fine. They buried him here in Dunkerque.

Well, I think I have told you all the news for this time. I have been in the best of health and hope you are in the same con-dition.

I am as ever,

Irving

---

[9]This is the end of page 9 of the letter. Page 10 is missing; and the letter picks up at the top of page 11.

{*When the U.S. Navy took over the French Naval Air Station at Dunkerque, it consisted of a few hangars facing the harbor, all of which sat on a stone quay elevated about ten feet above the water. To fly the antisubmarine patrols from that station, the Navy acquired a small fleet of French 200 hp Hispano-Suiza powered, Donnet-Denhaut flying boats.*

When not in use, the D-Ds and the pontooned Hanriot (HD-2) fighters sat on wheeled dollies atop the stone quay. When an aerial patrol was to take place, each plane had to be wheeled over to a stationary derrick, picked up, swung out off the quay, and lowered into the water.

The Dunkerque harbor, from where the D-D flying boats took off, was always congested with shipping, making either take-offs or landings dangerous undertakings. Naval Aviator Ens. George Moseley once tangled with the mast of a ship and crashed onto its deck but fortunately survived.

On the morning of May 6, 1918, between 8:42 and 8:45 a.m., two Donnet-Denhaut flying boats manned by U.S. Navy air crews, left NAS Dunkerque on an overwater, antisubmarine patrol. This patrol succeeded in becoming safely airborne, but twenty miles out over the North Sea, pilot Herbert Lasher, QR-1(A), put his D-D into a turn to make the next leg of the patrol, and the 200 hp Hisso engine stopped. The D-D went into a spin and crashed into the sea killing Observer Edward A. Smith, QR-1(A), and injuring Herbert Lasher and Thomas C. Holliday, QR-1(A). The second D-D landed on the water, picked up survivors, and stood by waiting for help. Pigeons carried messages to the station. At 10:50 and intervals until 12:09 two H.D.'s and the captain's launch left as rescue patrol. Visibility was poor, but the rescuing patrol returned with the captain's launch towing the 2nd D-D of the original patrol. Ensign Ingalls piloting a Hanriot of the rescuing patrol was reported missing, 4:00 to 8:00 p.m. Two D-D's left on patrol between 5:12 and 5:35 searching for Ensign Ingalls, and the captain's

Quay at NAS Dunkerque where the Donnet-Denhaut antisubmarine patrol flying boats had to be lifted by crane in and out of the water of the small bay. Accidents often occurred, with ships anchored or moored in the congested harbor, when Naval aviators tried to take off or land their waterborne aircraft. (Courtesy of Roger Sheely)

launch left at 5:30. Ensign Ingalls reported at 7:15 that he became lost and was safe at Le Havre. Visibility was only fair.

Herbert Lasher received a severly broken leg that mustered him out of the service and gave him problems the rest of his life.

It was at NAS Dunkerque that Irving met Ensign Kenneth MacLeish, Naval Aviator #74 and member of the famous First Yale Unit. In a letter to his family, MacLeish described the D-D accident that killed Smith and injured two others: "The rear observer saw what was coming, threw his (Lewis) guns overboard and braced himself for the shock. When he came to, he had a broken leg, but that was all. In that condition, he sent in three messages by pigeons, rescued the pilot, and dove for the front observer, but though he could touch him, couldn't clear him from the wreckage, and his body went down when the front half of the bus [flying boat] sank. The other machine [landed and] came to the rescue, and with five men on board started to sink. Two other machines and two scouts went out [from NAS Dunkerque], followed by another big machine. It reached the wreck and took all the load it could. One of the scouts arrived, saw what the situation was, brought two motor boats over, and just skinned into the harbor as his motor completely wrecked. Two of the three big rescuing machines collapsed before they got in. Only one of the seven machines came back without a mishap. Dave Ingalls was in one of the scouts, and left about ten in the morning. At five in the afternoon nothing had been heard from him. At seven nothing. Two big machines went out at seven, but came back with no news. Just then a telephone message came through stating that he was way down by Le Havre. He just hit the coast in time. A few more miles and he would have been out in the Atlantic Ocean."

(Log of U.S. NAS Dunkerque, France, May 6, 1918, National Archives, Washington, D.C.; Paine, The First Yale Unit, Vol. II; Herbert Lasher, Letter(s) written to L. Sheely; Ens. Herbert Lasher, Diary for May 6, 1918; Kenneth MacLeish, Kenneth: A Collection of Letters written by Lieut. Kenneth MacLeish, U.S.N.R.F.C.,

edited by Martha [Mrs. Andrew] MacLeish [Chicago: privately printed, 1919])}

U.S. Naval Air Station
Dunkerque, France
May 11, 1918

My Dear Mother,-

Altho I wrote only a short time ago I am going to celebrate "Mother's Day" as the government calls it.

As I understand it they will make a special effort to deliver all mail that is marked "Mother's Mail" and mailed tomorrow, in the least possible time.

I have received the letters from Laura and Lewis and also yours and am pleased with the way things are getting along.

I am glad the winter is over and I suppose you are too. I guess I can safely say it was about the mildest one I've been through. Of course its cold and disagreeable but its nothing compared to what we have in Albany.

In my last letter I told about my experience over the German lines and how ten Huns tried to get me. How they poured machine gun fire and bullets were whizzing about me and some of them piercing my wings.

Most of my flying at present is out over the North Sea. I have to get up at three o'clock tomorrow morning and make another patrol.

On the average I have to fly every other day.

It is so foggy over the sea that we have to navigate entirely by compass.

We carry four pigeons for messengers in case of motor trouble or accidents of any kind.

It is not yet a week ago [May 6, 1918] since one of these little messengers carried a sad message back to us. It was a call for help and quick.

I was the "Stand By" for the day and in a few minutes I was to the rescue.

"Stand By" is a saying or a name given to the one who should be ready to go in such cases.

We arrived on the scene just as the big flying boat was almost gone. All that was sticking out of the water was the tip of the tail. Poor "Red" Smith, for this is what we called him, was no more and we were helpless to try and get his body. We picked up Herbert Lasher and proceeded back in a hurry as he was in serious condition.

One leg broken and several cuts about the head and badly shaken up for he had fell over five hundred feet.

He is in the hospital now and is doing nicely.

I am going to send that clipping to him that Lewis sent to me. He will be pleased to see it.

He is sure a game kid for he is always talking about "Red" and never complains about himself. The other plane had to be towed in by a launch.

Night before last we had another all night session of it, which are getting to be quite often now.

I had gotten nice and soundly to sleep and being rather tired I guess, I never heard the siren which always blows when we have raids. The first thing I heard was B-O-O-M-B!!! and it nearly shook me out of bed. BOOMB!!! another bomb and I was tearing for the dugout while at the same time I was trying to get my pants on.

All the other fellows were "hitting the deck" too and they hit running.

When we emerged from the hut we found that the French had made such a smoke screen that we had to steer a course by dead reckoning to find the entrance.

One fellow paused to pull on a shoe and the fellow behind him tripped and fell headlong over him. Before they could get up a couple of more piled on top.

Anti-aircraft guns were roaring and scrapnel [sic] bursting and whizzing with that long wailing sound.

I have gotten up like this as many as eight and ten times in a night.

They also shell us from the sea and sometimes from the land. This land gun shoots a sixteen inch shell and I have been within thirty yards of where one of these shells broke.

This air raid I am telling about lasted till about one o'clock.

Turning in and getting to sleep again we were once more aroused. This time by the deep thundering roar of heavy guns at sea and we knew that another sea battle was in progress in close proximity.

They got going so strong that my bunk started to walk around the deck from the terrible shaking of the earth.

All these things I suppose seem quite exciting to you but they are getting to be quite common to us.

Well we managed to get a little over an hour's sleep when the bugle blew and if we are not on the minute we loose out on breakfast.

Guess you won't have any trouble getting me up for breakfast, like you used to, when I get back.

Its a year ago yesterday [May 10] that I left Pensacola, Florida for France.

I hope you have received my Insurance papers by now but I suppose the government has been pretty busy getting so many made out that it has been delayed.

As to the allotment that is for you, all of it. I have to pay fifteen of it and the government adds ten to it.

They have done this to help pay the expenses in homes where a member of the family is called away to war. In instances where a wife or mother is dependent. In your case it is that you were depending on my help to keep our home going. I enlisted and went away. I realized at the time and intended doing something as soon as possible. Which of course I did as you know.

I don't know exactly when this new one started but I know that on my last pay day I was checked for forty-five dollars. So you see that is three months anyway up to the end of April.

You will receive one more check of forty which is six checks in all and then that will be discontinued.

Didn't I tell you what the premium on the insurance was. Well it is only six dollars and sixty cents a month. Apres le Guerre fini they are going to make a way for us to continue this insurance if we wish to do so.

Yes, I have heard from Olive and have written quite a number of letters to her. She is anxious to hear from me but I only write when I feel inclined and that is not as often as it used to be.

However, if she had treated me different I would not feel so unconcerned. I'm sorry to hear about Aunt Lizzie and do hope she is better now. I owe a letter to Martha and I think I will have to "shake a leg" and catch up on my correspondence.

Well, I think I will close hoping this finds you well and happy as this leaves me that way. I am,

As Ever,

Irving

[*First Aeronautical Detachment veteran and now pilot, John Ganster QMM2, was flying an HD-2 (Hanriot fighter plane) over the city of Dunkerque on May 18, 1918, and while turning over the city, for some reason or reasons unknown, lost control and went into a nose dive. The seaplane struck the roof of a building on Rue Carnot, fell to the street, and burst into flames. Ganster was thrown clear of the machine. He was taken to a French military hospital and died at 9:45 a.m., another of the many wartime noncombat fatalities. (Log of U.S. NAS Dunkerque, France, spring 1918, National Archives, Washington, D.C.)]*

Dunkerque, France
May 19, 1918

Dear Friend Harry:- [?]

I know you will be surprised to have a letter from me but I intended writing to you many times but failed to get started at it.

I suppose you think because I'm so far away that I've forgotten all my friends but I haven't in the least.

I received the package from Scottie with your remembrance in it. I am more than thankful to you for it. It was a treat to taste American candy once more.

I wrote a little account of my first battle in the air, in Scottie's letter. I hope he has received it by this time and that you have read it. It was my first encounter with the Hun and I can assure you it was some exciting.

I landed on the aerodrome after being over the lines for two and a half hours. I looked the machine over and found several bullet holes in the fuselage and several more thru the wings.

Only one hole was traced that came very near being disastrous passing within a couple of inches of my leg. About a week ago one of our boys fell in the North Sea and was instantly killed. Yesterday we lost another. He fell about five hundred feet and was dashed to pieces. His motor baughted [*sic*] or failed him while flying over land. His machine being a seaplane was unable to make a landing. Both of these boys slept in the next bunks to me and I miss them terribly having been together for a long time. Its a dangerous game for we are getting bumped off fast. In fact there is only about half of us left that first came over, a year ago. We lost quite a number while in training.

The past two weeks I have done twenty two hours in the air.

Yesterday I flew three hours and was so tired that I never heard the air raid warning last night. Consequently the first thing I realized was a dreadful explosion and scrapnel [*sic*] whizzing. I hit the deck running too. The dugout is only a few yards away but it seems like a mile when a fellow is in such a hell of a hurry. Of course we lose a lot of sleep and grumble like blazes but never the less we stay in the dugout during an air raid.

We are sometimes shelled from the land and some from the sea, but mostly from the air.

Today is a beautiful day and the aeroplanes have been droning overhead all morning on their way to the front.

Its a pretty sight to see a squadron of machines flying in formation across the sky loaded with bombs on their way across the lines to destroy some objective in Germany. Then think and wonder if all of them will return.

I had a letter from Laura saying that she was expecting a ride on a motor cycle which you had promised to give her. She was very much pleased about it. Hope you don't get spilled in any tar.[10]

Just this moment one of the fellows came in and told us that Marshburn, another of our pilots, has fallen in a vrille [nose spin] and is killed.

This is sad news as he is a splendid fellow and a crack flyer. Something must have happened to his controls. Well Harry Old Boy, I must close, hoping to hear from you soon, I am

As Ever
Your friend
Irving

---

[10]In the pre-1917 years, road improvement consisted of just plain tar. Macadam and concrete had not yet come into widespread use.

[*Dunkerque pilot and Yale man, Navy Lt. Kenneth MacLeish, was chosen by another Yale man, Lt. Robert Lovett, to be a squadron commander in the forthcoming Northern Bombing Group. MacLeish chose Irving to be his observer, and they would be together for the next several months. Teams of pilots and observers were then sent in late May from Dunkerque to the U.S. Army Seventh Aviation Instruction Center at Clermont-Ferrand, in the Auvergne region of Central France, to receive squadron-level bombardment training.*

Training at Clermont-Ferrand lasted approximately four weeks, and during that time the subject of commissions for the enlisted observers was discussed in letters by Irving, MacLeish, and Ens. George C. Moseley, who also held his observer, Petty Officer Lowry, in high regard.

U.S. Navy pilot Ens. Moseley expressed his belief that commissions for the observers would allow the pilots to be more free with the observers and live in the same house with them. Officer rank for both would enable them to talk over the work, learn from their mistakes, and profit from the mistakes of others.

The question of commissions for these people continued unresolved until Navy directive T-50-M (NAV AIR 82-148) was issued by Cdr. Kenneth Whiting on February 3, 1919. It acknowledged that frequent inquiries had been made regarding commissions for enlisted observers. Whiting's response was that (1) the rating of observer does not exist and (2) enlisted men may be promoted or commissioned only in accordance with existing regulations.]

[*June saw a powerful German surprise ground attack against the French on the Aisne River; this attack drove a salient forty miles deep into the French positions and enabled the Germans to reach a point along the Marne River only thirty-seven miles from Paris. It was at Chateau-Thierry, in that sector, that the American Second Infantry Division, together with French troops, halted this advance.*]

[Irving wrote a note in the upper left-hand corner of this letter.]

Just this moment I have learned
that I have been recommended
for a commission. Wow! but
won't that be great. I rather felt
it coming.

U.S. Naval Air Service
#4 Place d' Iena
Paris, France
June 9, 1918

Dear Lewis

Received your letter of May 18 yesterday and glad to hear the good news.

Today is Sunday and I am trying to get all my mail answered but there is still about twenty letters waiting to be answered. I think I will decide on a little plan whereby I can eliminate some of this duplicate writing that I have been doing. Especially during these warm days when its so darn hot that a fellow nearly roasts sitting in the barracks trying to write letters.

If you are going to show all my letters around to people whats the use of writing things over and over again. The censor is strict so you see its rather hard to find something to write about.

However, I don't intend to slight anybody and if they think I'm doing so, why I'll just try and do the best I can.

I've been on the front for nearly three months and it isn't as soft as one would think. A fellows time to himself is limited. His sleep is uncertain and he is subject to orders at a minutes notice.

However, there are times when the battle lulls for a while and we get a chance to do something for ourselves. It is generally consumed by doing our washing, writing, shaving and taking a bath, (not always possible) and such things.

I will give you a list of names that have told me they read my letters from home Shrieves, Clapham, Forner and the people in New York. I will write them if possible and as soon as I can, but I will write the first letter home as I have been doing and if the rest get a chance why alls well.

I have started writing duplicates but you have found me out so that didn't work.

I suppose you will be surprised to hear where I am at present. I am at Clermont-Ferrand training on avions.[11]

Heretofore I have been flying in hydroavions. Believe me I'm glad too because I hate those old seaplanes. Also its darned tiresome flying over water all the time. Also I don't fancy a watery grave like four of our number have already gone to.

One which Herb Lasher came very near going to. He is recovering nicely now. I sent him that clipping you sent me and he was very much pleased about it.

My work will be bombing from high altitudes exceedingly dangerous but interesting and exciting.

I wish you could imagine a picture of a squadron of aeroplanes loaded with bombs and machine guns flying in V formation on their way across the lines carrying destruction under their sturdy wings.

---

[11]The French two-seat Breguet Type 14 B.2 day-bomber, powered with one 300-hp 12-cylinder Renault, carried a bomb load of 660 lbs at a speed of 115 mph. It was first delivered in 1917 and served l'Armée de l'Air until 1930. It was never as popular with the Americans as the Liberty-powered DH-4. One significant feature of this sturdy aircraft was the extensive use of both aluminum and steel in its construction. (Thetford, *Aircraft of the 1914–1918 War*, pp. 67–68)

Now you can realize that your brother has been selected to fly in the foremost plane as squadron commander's picked man.

```
        +   <————This is the position
    +       +       I am referring to.
  +               +
  +                   +
```

Well its so.

I hope I'll be able to fulfill my important position.

I have several good tactics which will help me wonderful in this new work.

First of all and best, is that, I am fearless in the air. I understand my machine gun and know thoroughly what it can do. I know how to use it. And best of all I feel confident to hold my own against the Hun.

If America turns out the planes and supplies and accessories such as machine guns, ammunition, bombs, etc. we will do disastrous work against the enemy in the near future.

I had a letter from Frank telling me all about what he had been doing. Glad to hear about yourself and hope you will hold it down, as it sounds like good work.

Seems as tho the old home has been turned upside down the past year, don't it?

I am sure glad I'm in aviation and just think I've got you to thank for it.[12]

Casualties are coming in heavy with the American Army and I'm glad I am not in those trenches as from what I've seen of the men that came back from the front, they lead the life of a dog.

---

[12]With the death of his father in 1911, it is apparent that Irving turned to his younger brother, Lewis, for counsel before deciding to join Naval Aviation.

How did you learn to run a car? It sure does make me a little homesick to hear the names of those little towns you speak of.

You see in my line I don't pay any attention to roads, bridges, or such things. I'm afraid I would be running cross-lots with a car if I were to go anywhere.

I'd like to give you a race with your bus. Guess I could run rings around you, Eh, what?

I can only throttle down to about seventy per and open up to a hundred and thirty.

How would you like to ride as fast as that once?

I had a letter from my little French friend a few days ago and I think I will enclose it as it might amuse you. It took me about a week to read it and understand it thoroughly.

However, I have quite a lot of amusement corresponding with her. Elle est tres jollie fille. Just notice what she wants me to be. I have to laugh about it as it seems rather funny to me.

I haven't received those packages yet and I don't expect I ever will. Of course I'm sorry about them but at present I am not in want for anything.

Are you getting my allotment right along? There should have been six payments of forty and then fini.

I don't know exactly when the new one started but I know that the first time they took out for it was three months back and that is two or three months ago.

Let me know exactly what you have received so I can keep track of it.

Well, I think I have told you all for this time. Hoping this finds you all well.

I am

as ever,

Irving

[No date, estimate mid-June 1918]

Dear Brother Scottie:-

After a little over three months on the front in which I have succeeded in proving very good work, I have been selected with a few others to take a special course in high altitude bombing. Therefore you will understand why I am at Clermont-Ferrand, almost in the central part of France.

It's a very beautiful place situated in a broad valley surrounded by mountains. Of course you know how I like the hills and country. It's just like a vacation considering what we went through at Dunkerque, no air raids, no seventeen inch shells bursting around us, able to sleep all night unmolested and good grub. Wow, but you can't guess how I am enjoying it.

Pretty little French girls to go promenading with occasionally. It seems as if life is worth living for after all.

We have to fly about three hours a day and then the rest is to ourselves. I'm sorry it is only going to last a month and a half.

I will try and tell you briefly what our work will consist of. It is called by the English, High Altitude Day Light Bombing. This is flying in a formation of from five to eleven machines at an altitude of 20,000 feet far into German territory and dropping bombs on their factories, railroad centers, ammunition depots, etc.

You may imagine what hazardous work this may be.

I have watched the English time and time again go over in the famous duck and geese formation, flying to some objective in Germany and carrying destruction neath their sturdy wings. Can you imagine such a sight? Then think and wonder how many will ever return.

I will tell you a little about our first small squadron we are forming and training at present. First and best of all is that your Uncle Dudley [Irving] has been picked to fly in the squadron

Commanders machine. This is the leading machine and he is responsible for the whole squadron. That he is to do the navigating and lead them to the objective, do the sighting and then giving the signal which the other planes upon seeing immediately release all their bombs. This doesn't seem like very much to do but if you could understand how difficult they are to do in the air, you may be sure that it is some job.[13]

Some more good news, within the past week I was told by our officer that I have been recommended for a commission. Hot Dog but you can bet *I'm tickled*. It's pretty nice to know that your hard work is being appreciated.

I am going to enclose a little clipping written in a paper called "Flights and Landings" that the boys have written about some of us. Although being greatly exaggerated, they have a little truth about them.

I have been working on a little invention which I hope will pan out pretty good. If I am successful it will play H— with the dutchmen.

---

[13]While at Clermont-Ferrand, Ens. Moseley described his work as pilot and that of his observer, Petty Officer George Lowry. Lowry trained with Irving in England and also served in RAF 202 Squadron. Moseley said that he was glad that his observer not only was a good shot with bombs, but also was a wonder with a machine gun. At an altitude of 1,200 meters, they found the little white circle on the ground, the target, headed directly into the wind, and began to drive over it. Lowry watched the ground through his instrument. If they drifted a little to the right, Lowry would pull a line that was attached to Moseley's left arm, and he would gradually turn the machine to the left, until receiving a sharp jerk on his right arm. Moseley would hold that course until crossing the target. The observer had a very hard job, Moseley explained. The pilots flew once as observer so that they could develop a higher form of teamwork, as the pilot is apt to think that the observer has nothing to do but ride. (George Clark Moseley, *Extracts from the Letters of George Clark Moseley, During the Period of the Great War*, 1923)

However, I'm working under difficulties. They all kid me about it calling me such names as Edison, Maxim, and even going so far as to put such stuff in the paper. I suppose you will say "It's just like him" or something to that effect, too. Well, you know, old man, we've got to win this 'ere war, and I reckon as how'r every little bit helps. N'est-ce-pas?[14]

Upon completing our course we expect to go to Bordeaux and fly American machines from there to our aerodrome in the vicinity of Dunkerque. How would you like to make that trip in an aeroplane? On our way we hope to fly over Paris.

Your letter dated May 25th reached me today and I thought it was very good time making the trip across, a little less than a month you see. I am exceeding pleased that you have let all my friends read my letters, as I know they are glad to hear something about what I am doing.

I was delighted with the letter as it contained a word from all the boys. It would have done you good to see me read it, as I grinned and chuckled to myself and wishing I could count the days when I could see them all once more.

Well, Scottie rest assured I will match my utmost ability against the Hun. However if I fail you may be sure I go down fighting desperate. From what I hear and read this is the spirit with our boys on the front and in the air. At first I understand that the average American fell for this "Kamerad" stuff. I'm finding

---

[14]Irving called upon the college-trained MacLeish to do some of the calculations associated with the optics that he and his machinist mate pal, Randall R. Browne, observer for Lt. David Ingalls, wished to redesign. MacLeish referred to Irving as his "HE observer" who had invented a modification for a bombsight whereby one cannot miss the target, adding that it was perfectly marvelous. Later, MacLeish praised Irving's bombing capability saying: "My Observer is THERE. He made 3 direct hits in three passages from 1200 meters, the best done before was two out of three."

him out to be just as treacherous as before, the Americans have no mercy on the dutchman that shouts Kamerad. Thus he has come to fear the American boys. Notice this little clipping I will enclose concerning this.

Hoping I may hear from you soon. I will close for this time. Give my regards to all the boys.

I am, as ever

Your Brother

Irving

[*While at Clermont-Ferrand, Irving and several others witnessed one of the most bizarre nonfatal mishaps in aviation's early history.*

Army pilot 1st Lt. Samuel Pierce Mandell and his observer 1st Lt. Gardiner H. Fiske were engaged in aerial gunnery practice aboard a Breguet aircraft. Mandell related that they were flying formation in these buses and his machine had two camera guns on it, one for the pilot and one for the observer. Lt. Fiske was standing up on the seat in back, shooting his camera gun at a scout machine that was flying around them. Mandell dove to get a shot at him with his forward gun. He heard a crash behind, and a man in a leather coat was holding onto the tail of his machine. Fiske had fallen out of his cockpit when his gun broke loose from its fastening. Mandell put the machine in the gentlest glide and started for home as they were at an altitude of 2300 feet. Fiske was lying with his body across the fuselage, in front of the vertical stabilizer on the tail.

Fiske slowly worked his way up the fuselage by jamming his hands through the fabric and grabbing a structural member of the aircraft; finally he caught hold of the tourelle at the edge of the cockpit from which he had been ejected and dove head first into his seat with only his heels sticking out. All the time it was happening they were flying at a minimum of 100 mph. Irving referred to having witnessed this event in his July 25, 1918 letter to his sister, Laura.

Lt. Gardiner H. Fiske was later posted to the 20th Aero Bombard-

ment Squadron as an observer on August 31, 1918. He was the lead observer during the last air raid by the 20th on November 5, 1918, and survived the war.

Lt. Samuel P. Mandell was assigned to the 20th Aero Squadron on August 30, 1918. He, too, participated in the November 5, 1918 aerial attack on Mouzon. His Liberty-powered, American-made DH-4 was shot up and fell to the ground at Martincourt. Lt. R. W. Fulton, of New York, his observer, was practically unhurt; Mandell's leg was badly broken in the crash landing. The Germans marched Fulton away and left the wounded pilot propped up against his plane. About 4 o'clock in the afternoon, a German captain of infantry came to the site of the wrecked aircraft, saw the wounded American, took a rifle from one of the German guards, and deliberately fired a number of shots into the helpless Lt. Mandell. His body was found on November 17, 1918, by a detachment of the 5th U.S. Marine Infantry and after initial burial nearby was reinterred at a little U.S. military cemetery between Beaumont and Letanne, France.

(Marvin L. Skelton, "Recollections of 1st Lt. Karl C. Payne, No. 20 Aero Squadron, U.S.A.S.," Cross & Cockade Journal [Society of WWI Aero Historians] 21, No. 4 [1980], pp. 307–10)]

> U.S. Naval Air Service
> 4 Place d' Iena
> Paris, France
> June 26, 1918

Dear Olive,-

I am not sure whether I answered your last letter or not.

I have been on the front for a little over three months and I know you will excuse me for being so neglectful.

It has passed the year mark since I landed in France and there has been many things happened during that time. I have flown over the lines far into the enemy territory, had my first battle in the air far above the clouds. I have faced death squarely in the face and not faltered. If I had failed to do my duty I would have been lost. Can you imagine me climbing into my machine and realize what my mission is? Being comfortably seated then whizz away into space to do my little part in this great war.

This is every day life to me and my heart beats steady all the time. God grants me courage and I feel perfectly safe in his keeping.

I have been selected to do some special kind of work after proving to be capable while at the front.

At present I am at Clermont-Ferrand training in this new work and expect to be back at the front in a short time. Its a beautiful place, situated in the central part of France surrounded by mountains. They remind me of the country around Middleburg [N.Y.] and you can just guess I'm enjoying it too.

I am flying in land machines instead of seaplanes and I like them much better. My work will be what the English call daylight bombing. This is flying at an altitude of about twenty thousand feet over the enemy territory and dropping bombs on German factories, railroads, and all such important objectives. This is very hazardous work as the Huns are fighting you off with their aeroplanes and firing at you with anti-aircraft guns trying to shoot you down. However, its exciting and wherever there is something doing I want to be in it if its possible to get there.

Olive, I am more than pleased with your letters and do hope you will continue to write even though I am unable to answer them promptly. They cheer me up immensely, make me think of home and that there is a place in this world somewhere where there is no thoughts of killing and work of destruction being wrought.

I like the pictures you sent and think you are an excellent amature. I imagine you to be quite a young lady now considering it has been nearly two years since I've seen you. I am going to write a sentence in French about you so Mamma and Papa can't read it. I'll fool them, understand?

Vous etes une tres belle petite fille.

I hope you have passed all your examinations by this time as you said in your letter that you were just taking them. Does Dorothy have tests this year too? How I wish I could come back for a visit. I would fly over Cotton Hill and land in that nice field just in from the house and surprise you.

However, I'll have to stop dreaming for I'm apt to get homesick.

Hoping this finds you all well and happy and that I will hear from you again soon.

I am as ever,
Irving

CHAPTER 6

Lt. MacLeish, the RAF, and the NBG

July 3 to August 24, 1918

[*During June and July, the Second Battle of the Marne was fought with the Germans successfully crossing the river in two places. Once across, however, German progress was halted by both French and Americans with the latter fighting the famous battle of Belleau Wood during that period. The German ground offensive was spent. On July 18, General Foch ordered a counterattack, which drove the Germans back across the Marne, and the Allied initiative, begun on that date, was sustained throughout the balance of the fighting.*

On July 3, 1918, a small group of sailors arrived in a wheat field near the town of St. Ingleverte, four and a half miles west of Calais, and five miles inland from the English Channel. Their mission was to start construction of a supply distribution base in support of the Northern Bombing Group. These men experienced and surmounted privations and great difficulties. (Frederick N. Bolle, The Battle of Eastleigh *[U.S.N.A.F., 1919], p. 86)*]

US Naval Air Service
4 Place d' Iena
Paris, France
July 3, 1918

Dear Lewis,-

Suppose you will be surprised to receive this letter from Paris but I am on my way to the front again, having spent the day here between trains.[1]

I think this is my seventh time in the great city.

There isn't much news except that we will be operating in the North West Bombing section.[2]

You may bet I'm glad to be able to get a chance to give those Huns some of their own medicine. I've run to the dugout a great many times and I will think of these times when I am flying over their ground and say to myself, "Run you son of a guns! I'm going to pull the release and let some bombs bust on your tail!"

Well, I will probably know more about things in a couple of weeks. We are leaving tonight on the nine o'clock train and will arrive there at Dunkirk tomorrow morning about six o'clock. Its a tiresome journey. We have to sit up all the way. In fact I have never seen a sleeper or anything like one while in France.

Most of our traveling has been at night owing to conditions. I have made this trip five times to Dunkirk and believe me I know whats ahead of me.

While at the Y.M.C.A. today I was getting a check cashed and a fellow asked me if I was sending any home. I told him I'd like to but as yet I hadn't found a very convenient way of doing so.

Well he showed me all about the Y's way and I concluded that it was very good and exceedingly safe. So am sending Mamma two hundred dollars 200$\underline{^{00}}$ which if she will, put it in the bank for me.

I will try and send some more soon. My pocket book is swelling up you see. Of course I'm keeping a good amount in

---

[1]Despite the contents of this letter, the original 1918 envelope still exists containing a square blue stamp that says, "Passed Censor." Censoring was done for the most part by the flying officers, and they refer to it in their letters home as just another "chore."

[2]Northern Bombing Group is the official title for the operation.

case of an emergency. I also have about $300 in the bank at Bordeaux and about $200 left in my pocket.

I hope you are getting the allotment all right. Wish you would state this in some of your letters. You have never told me that you received the last one of forty dollars yet. I hope you won't forget this. I received your last letter while at Clermont-Ferrand a day or two ago.

I am glad to hear of your good work at college.

By the way Herbert Lasher is commissioned and he is coming back to America on furlough.[3] It will be a long time before he will be able to walk again and perhaps rendering him unable to fly any more.

I'll say he is a lucky boy. What do you think? Wish I could imagine myself going back to America on a furlough and with a commission.

Well, its nearly time for me to take the Metro (subway) for Gare du Nord and departie pour Dunkerque. Compreney vous?

As I can't think of any more to write I will close hoping to hear from you soon. I am as ever,

Irving

P.S. don't forget to let me know immediately on the receipt of the check for the 200. N'est cepas?

[*The NAS Dunkerque station log for July 8, 1918 stated that the following officers and men were to be transferred to #218 Squadron RAF for temporary duty in connection with day bombing: Lt. K. MacLeish, Lt. D. Ingalls, Ens. D. E. Judd, R. R. Browne (MM1C), S. L. Huey (QM1C) and I. E. Sheely (MM1C). The log also noted that the body of Eichelberger, killed in a seaplane accident along with Ens. Curtis Read on February 26, 1918, was reported recovered off the coast of France near*

---

[3]Those of the First Aeronautical Detachment who went through pilot training at Tours were usually commissioned. (Van Wyen, *Naval Aviation in WWI*, p. 14)

Ensign Kenneth MacLeish, Naval Aviator #74, often Irving's pilot, was killed in air combat October 14, 1918, over Schoore, Belgium, while attached to RAF #213 Squadron. (Courtesy of Roger Sheely)

La Panne and sent to La Martine hospital to be prepared for burial. These entries were signed by L. A. De Sonier, Ens., USN (Naval Aviator #762 and another First Aeronautical Detachment veteran).]

U.S. Naval Air Station
Dunkerque, France
July 8, 1918

Dear Mother,-

I have again arrived on the old battlefront and believe me we were gladly received. The first night we had a severe raid but last night was one of the worst I've ever been thru.

The ground trembled like an earthquake and the scrapnel [*sic*] was whizzing around like hailstones. Of course I can't tell you the material damage it did to us but you may be sure we are not left out.

One of the first bombs dropped set fire in a certain section and the illumination enabled the night raiders to hammer the pudding out of us.

However, our time is coming as in the very near future, perhaps a couple of weeks I hope to be doing the same thing to them.

I wrote to Lewis while in Paris and I am going to ask a few things over in case it doesn't reach you.

First I have sent a check of two hundred dollars thru the Y.M.C.A. to you. If your absolutely in need of any of this, use it. If not will you put it in the bank for me.

I am saving enough here in case anything happens to me.

Also will you please let me know about the allotment if you have received the last check of forty or not. And if you are getting the new one right along.

You see I am paying for this and I have no way of knowing whether you are receiving it, except from you. Also let me know about the insurance papers.

I had a very nice time while I was training in central France. It was a beautiful country and well away from the war zone. I met some American soldiers that were wounded and they told some vivid stories of their experiences. Met one fellow from Albany. He had worked in the Albany Garage previous to enlisting. He knew Walter Gee [?] and said that Walter was now among the American fighting forces in France.

I haven't heard from Settone lately but I have been told that he has been on a seven day leave at Aix de Bains.

You probably know that they will not let us have leave in Paris anymore. I am quite sorry about this as I like Paris better than New York City. I have been in quite a number of large cities including London and I don't know of any I like so well as Paris.

My leave is due but I think I will wait till a little later and take a trip to southern France.

We are allowed seven days which is not half bad. N'est ce pas? I think this will continue every four months.

How is Mr. Smith, yourself and all the rest of the folks?

Herb Lasher is an Ensign and is on his way home. He has been gone about two weeks.

Hope Lewis will be able to see him.

He will no doubt visit Schenectady and old Union College.

Well, I think I will close hoping to hear from you soon.

> I am as ever
> Irving

[*On June 3 the RAF added the 82nd Wing to the 5th Group. It was responsible for day and night bombing exclusively and consisted of: 38 Squadron, 214 Squadron, and 218 Squadron. RAF 218 Squadron operated DeHavilland DH-9, a single-engine bomber aircraft. The DH-9 was intended to be the 1918 replacement for the hard-working DH-4, but it proved to be far less than a suitable replacement.*

On July 6, 1918, constant enemy night raids upon Dunkerque forced 218 Squadron to move its base farther from the front. The leaders chose an aerodrome at Fretnum in the immediate southwest environs of Calais, twenty-four miles west of Dunkerque. From Fretnum 218 continued constant aerial bombardment of the submarine targets at Ostende, Bruges, and Zeebrugge.

On July 9, 1918, S. L. Huey, I. E. Sheely, and R. R. Browne left NAS Dunkerque to report for temporary duty at 218 Squadron.

Lt. MacLeish described some of the difficulties he and Sheely had on a raid they flew as pilot and observer respectively in DH-9 #1206 on July 16th. The flight from Fretnum to the target was uneventful, but once there, they discovered nine Hun aircraft were ready to dive on them but stayed back because "Archie" (ground antiaircraft) was exploding all around the RAF bombers.

Their DH-9 took a hit from that antiaircraft fire but not a full one. It hit under the tail of the "bus," and the DH-9 went into all kinds of dives before MacLeish could regain control. Both flyers were probably shaken by the near fatal strike. They looked at each other, but neither said anything in particular.

Just as MacLeish pulled out of the dive, the motor quit cold. There were thirty miles to go before crossing the lines, and a forty or fifty mph wind to fly into. Just then the engine began to sputter and gurgle and then caught on five cylinders. They came those thirty miles against that wind on five cylinders, and it took them fifty-five minutes.

DH-9 aircraft #1206 was probably powered by a 230 hp Siddeley "Puma." This was an in-line six cylinder engine originally designed by Beardmore, Halford, Pullinger (BHP) and licensed to Siddeley-Deasy Motors (England) for production. By all standards this engine was a "dog," especially when compared to the 360 hp geared down Rolls-Royce "Eagle VIII" of the same period and used successfully in the DH-4, which the DH-9 was intended to replace. Former US Army Air Service Lt. Oliver Hall flew many photo reconnaissance missions over the

DH-9 bomber flown by RAF 218 Squadron in which Irving flew three bombing missions with U.S. Naval Aviator Lt. Kenneth MacLeish. On April 12, 1918, while attached to RAF #202 Squadron, Irving, as rear observer/gunner for a British pilot, Coulthard, engaged a flight of German Albatros fighters. (Artist Simpson; Courtesy of The Trustees of the Imperial War Museum, London)

Zeebrugge-Ostend area for RAF 202 Squadron in his Eagle VIII powered DH-4 and always gave it the highest praise.

Those who wrote the history of the DH-9 aircraft agree that if it had any success, it was due entirely to the courage and determination of the pilots and observers who flew in them. The vulnerability of the DH-9 is hinted at by an average true air speed, flying level at 13,000 ft. at about 76 mph with bombs and 85 mph without bombs.

There was one major improvement in the DH-9 over the DH-4 that may appear trivial but was significant to both pilot and observer. The pilot and the observer cockpits were widely separated in the DH-4, so voice communication was almost impossible. The DH-9 moved the pilot back, out from under the overhead wing, locating his cockpit just in front of that of the observer/gunner.

The close proximity of the pilot and observer in the DH-9 was carried over into the later, 400 hp Liberty-powered DH-9A. Otherwise the DH-9A was hard to distinguish from the DH-4.

During an interview shortly before his death in 1974, David Judd complained that the pilot was overworked in a DH-9. All his gunlayer had to do was fire the Lewis machine gun from the aft cockpit while the pilot had to fly the plane and drop the bombs. Despite the disparaging remarks of others, Lt. Judd characterized the DH-9 as "A fine little sewing machine."]

RAF SQUADRON RECORD BOOK

Date: 16 July 1918	Duty: Air Raid		No. 218 Squadron	
			Hour of:	
Type & No.	Pilot	Observer	Start	Return
DH-9 6250	Capt. Chisholm,	G/L Williams	1035	1310
DH-9 1294	Lt. Judd,	2/Lt. Huey	1035	1315
DH-9 1206	Lt. McLeish,	M. M. Shelley	1035	1335
DH-9 3099	Lt. Stata,	2/Lt. Browne	1035	1330
DH-9 7673	Lt. Pugh,	2/Lt. Ankers	1035	Missing

[*There was a total of 13 DH-9 aircraft on this raid. Note the misspelling of "MacLeish" and "Sheely" and the 2/Lt. applied to U.S. Navy QM1/C Huey. The 2/Lt. Browne was a British Officer and not USN MM1/C Randall R. Browne. See flight of July 20, 1918.*]

Pilot Report on Bomb Dropping: Objective: Zeebrugge Mole Harbour and Workships.
DH-9 1206 Lt. McLeish USA 4 x 50 lb. bombs from 13000 ft. with four bursts. *Remarks:* in the sea.

RAF SQUADRON RECORD BOOK

Date: 19 July 1918   *Duty: Air Raid*   *No. 218 Squadron*

| | | | Hour of: | |
Type & No.	Pilot	Observer	Start	Return
DH-9 6250	Capt. Chisholm,	G/L Williams	0700	0940
DH-9 1294	Lt. Judd,	M. M. Huey	0700	0945
DH-9 3094	Lt. McLeish,	M. M. Shelley	0700	0955
DH-9 3099	Lt. Stata,	2/Lt. Browne	0700	0950

[*Because of the loss of one aircraft on the raid of the 16th, this raid consisted of 12 aircraft.*]

Pilot Report on Bomb Dropping: [totally illegible]

RAF SQUADRON RECORD BOOK

Date: 20 July 1918   *Duty: Air Raid*   *No. 218 Squadron*

| | | | Hour of: | |
Type & No.	Pilot	Observer	Start	Return
DH-9 1294	Lt. Judd,	M. M. Huey	0655	0940
DH-9 3094	Lt. McLeish,	M. M. Shelley	0655	0940
DH-9 3099	Lt. Stata,	2/Lt. Browne	0655	0935
DH-9 7628	Lt. Ingalls,	M. M. Browne	0655	0935

[*There was a total of 11 DH-9 aircraft on this raid. Finally got everybody rated correctly.*]

Pilot Report on Bomb Dropping:
DH-9 3094 Lt. McLeish 8 x 25 lb. Cooper, 8 bursts. At mouth of
        canal close to 3 Dredgers and 1 T.B.D. Observed 2 ships
        anchored between Blankenberghe and Ostende. 2 ex-
        plosions on Blockships outside Ostend. A large steamer
        entering Ostend Harbour.

[*On July 23, 1918, Lt. Godfrey deC. Chevalier relinquished command
at NAS Dunkerque and assumed command at the recently acquired
Assembly and Repair Base at Eastleigh, England. Eastleigh is on the
south coast just north of the major port city of Southampton. It was to be
the alternative site for the Northern Bombing Group Supply Distribution Base then at St. Ingleverte, France. During the June 1918 period,
it was considered a distinct possibility that the Hun might yet overrun the
Pas de Calais area, so it was imperative to relocate such an important
logistics base across the channel in England.*]

> U.S. Naval Air Service
> Dunkerque, France
> July 25, 1918

Dear Laura,-

Received your letter and also Mamma's yesterday and as I am
not flying today I will try and answer it right away.

I have been across the lines four times now, three times on
bombing trips.

Anti-aircraft fire is very active when we go over and scrapnel
[*sic*] flies around us rather abundantly.

My first bombing trip one of these shells burst just beneath my
tail. A piece of scrapnel went thru the rudder. You may be sure my
old boat rocked a little also. However, one of my least worries is
falling out of my machine, altho I have seen two cases where it has
happened. Once at St. Raphael a Frenchman was thrown out and
was killed. Another time only a short time ago at Clermont-

Ferrand an Army man was thrown out but he landed on the tail of his machine and crawled back in. This is an absolute fact as I see it myself. The poor fellow was somewhat frightened but he didn't loose his nerve.

Well, I was telling about bombing three times. I've made the Huns run to the dugouts. Of course I can't see them being so high up but just the same I know their going as they know we are going to drop bombs very quickly.

It takes about thirty seconds for them to fall and I try and watch them explode.

Well, then I wonder how many Huns they catch napping and blow up and also the damage they do to the buildings.

Of course this is hard to think about but they come over and do the same thing to us.

Well, I see you have made quite a number of changes especially in the line of jobs. How do you like your new position? I think Alice is doing fine. Does she like it too? Mamma's letter had a lot of good news in it. I am glad she has received the insurance policy.

As for the Knickerbocker Press which she said she was going to send. It is hardly worth while as they don't pay much attention to second class matter and I probably wouldn't get it half the time. Therefore, I wish she would not bother with it.

I know a better idea. If there is anything that is or would be interesting cut it out and send the clipping.

Don't you think that is a better plan?

I had a letter from Martha telling me she and Aunt Lizzie were down.

I am sorry to hear that she is not feeling well and hope that she gets better quickly.

Settone wrote me a few days ago and said he is not seeing very much of the war.

I did not know that you had received that picture from Pensacola. Why didn't you tell me about it before?

You know I've never seen it as it was taken the night before we left there.

Another fellow from Albany I think he is in the picture sent it for me.

Jimmy Smith lies in a little cemetery just outside the city of Dunkerque. I went to the funeral, the first military funeral I've been to. It was very impressive and never will forget it. As for myself I couldn't ask for better honor than was given to Smith.[4]

The firing squad which fired the military salute over his body, the taps which was blown by the bugler all tended to make us feel the loss of a comrade and friend.

There is nothing which Mrs. Smith can do in the way of Jimmy's request.

In fact it wasn't a request. He simply talked about his eagerness to fly.

He talked about his mother and sister previous to his death but had nothing to ask of them. There was nothing he wanted to be done.

This news or information was given to me by the little hospital attendant who did everything possible for him to the last. Jimmy was a friend of everybody and his passing away was deeply felt by all in camp.

If there is anything I can do or information I can give to either his mother or lady friend I will be glad to do so.[5]

---

[4]The identity of "Jimmy Smith" might have been revealed in the missing page 10 of Irving's letter of April 29, 1918. Irving said in the one sentence on page 11, "They buried him in Dunkerque."

[5]Irving's handwriting was noticeably shaky with a lot of mistakes and crossouts.

I have sent two hundred dollars home thru the YMCA and hope you will let me know as soon as you receive it.

Hoping this finds you all well,

I am

As Ever

Irving

[*Planning for the U.S. Navy Northern Bombing Group was well under way in the spring of 1918. It was to be the first Navy strategic bombing force. Its primary mission was to carry and drop heavy ordnance on the reinforced concrete submarine pens in German-occupied Belgium in hopes that such attacks would be powerful enough to take the U-boat out of the war.*

Much to the chagrin of the Naval aviators, the Marine aviators firmly established themselves as the Day Wing. The Marine wing did operate DH-4 bombers, and their first raid in force was made by eight planes of Marine Squadron 9 on the railroad junction at Thielt, Belgium. On that raid 2nd Lt. Ralph Talbot and his observer, GySgt. R. G. Robinson, both earned the Medal of Honor.

Thus the Navy became the Night Wing. In the absence of available American bomber aircraft, the Navy attempted to obtain the huge, twin-engine Handley-Page 0/400, but because of their few numbers, the RAF was understandably reluctant to part with them. The RAF graciously allowed Navy Lt. Cdr. Robert Lovett to accompany an RAF H-P squadron as an observer, but this state-of-the-art bomber was not for sale or even loan at that time.

Instead, contracts were let in Italy for the three-engine Caproni heavy bombers, and Navy pilots were sent there to ferry them over the Alps to a NBG aerodrome at St. Ingleverte. The aircraft of Italian Count Caproni di Taliedo along with the Handley-Page of Britain and the Gotha of Germany were three well-known multiengine aircraft of World

*War I. The Ca. 5 series, model 44 Caproni, mounted a pusher engine at
the rear of its short central fuselage. Twin booms running back to the tail
each contained a tractor engine. All three were six-cylinder, inline, water-
cooled 200/300 hp Fiat A-12bis engines. Besides being hand-fitted,
which did not permit parts replacement, the Fiat had, on several
occasions, ignited escaping fuel while in the air, with disastrous results.*

*Delivery of the Caproni to the Navy in northern France was slow.
When they did arrive, the Fiats required a lot of rework to prepare them
for reliable operation on the combat missions of the Northern Bombing
Group.*

*Lt. MacLeish was scheduled to be one of the Night Wing squadron
commanders with Petty Officer Sheely as his observer.*

*Independent offensive operations by the U.S. Navy's Northern
Bombing Group began at nine o'clock on the evening of August 15,
1918, when a Caproni bomber, piloted by Ens. L. R. Taber of Air
Squadron 1 with Ens. Chas. Fahy as copilot and D. C. Hale, rear
gunner, took off from St. Ingleverte. The German submarine repair docks
at Ostende, Belgium, were the objective, and they succeeded in dropping
1,650 pounds of explosives, registering two direct hits. Unfortunately
this same plane, on a later trip, got mixed up with a barrage battery, with
the inevitable result.*

*The Fiat engines were so bad that an order went to Italy for
replacement with the more reliable Isotta-Fraschini engine. These did not
arrive in numbers before the cessation of hostilities. The delays inspired the
derisive reference to the Northern Bombing Group by the British as "No
Bloody Good." After the Armistice, Navy personnel took great pleasure
in burning the Capronis.*

*(Log of the USNA Northern Bombing Group, National Archives,
Washington, D.C.; Van Wyen, Naval Aviation in WWI, pp. 84-87;
Munson, Bombers, Patrol and Reconnaissance Aircraft 1914–
1919, p. 157; Lamberton, Reconnaissance and Bomber Aircraft of
the 1914–1918 War, p. 148; Smith, Aircraft Piston Engines,*

Irving captioned this photo, "Caproni bombing plane about to start on a raid into the enemy territory from the Northern Bombing Group aerodrome at St. Inglevert, France." (Courtesy of Roger Sheely)

p. 41; Paine, The First Yale Unit, *Vol. II, pp. 181–89, 213–41, 263, 267)*

U.S.N.A.F.
Northern Bombing Group
Field A, France
Aug. 24, 1918

Dear Mother,-

I received your most interesting letter of july 28 and very glad to hear all the good news.

Of course you're kidding about my mustache but wait till you see the top of my dome.

I can begin to count 'em now. However, I've done everything to save my hair but without success.

Perhaps its the speed I travel through the air that is the cause of it.

Well, since I've been back at the front I have been over the lines three times.

Anti-aircraft guns are very active all the time we are over the enemy territory and scrapnel [*sic*] is flying around you very abundantly. I had several pieces go thru my tail and some thru my wings.

We seldom pay any attention to scrapnel as long as it doesn't hit us or some vital part of the engine.

We drop our bombs and watch them hit then come on home. On passing over the trenches if an opportunity is possible we open up our machine guns and pour the bullets into the Huns and shake them up a bit.

Yesterday I had a big washing to do and maybe you think I can't scrub clothes. I've got it down to a science now the same as I have patching and sewing on buttons.

However, I don't think I would mind having some of that stuff they call "No Rub" and perhaps I could economize on elbow grease, which is not very plentiful owing to the limited amount of chow.

I had a letter from Mr. Clapham and he asked how I would like to enjoy some nice fresh corn on the cob that he was going to have for dinner. Yes, and I thought of a lot more things including nifley and domies that I'd like to get on the outside of.[6]

However, I have been feeling fine, also look healthy enough. I don't know what I weigh. The last time was while I was in England. Then I weighed something like 14 stone (or bricks). It didn't make much difference for I didn't take time to figure out how many pounds that was.

I had to laugh at the way you spoke about Mr. Smith saying that he thought he was about twenty pounds shy too.

These slim fellows make good aviators as they afford a small target and are less apt to be hit by scrapnel or bullets. Why not be an aviator and get to France!!!

I was quite surprised to hear about Ermandine's [cousin] wedding. I hope she doesn't have the experience of loosing her hubby like so many of the other girls have. Get married then get drafted and go to war.

Seems as though all the girls I know are getting married. There's F. Rockenstire and several others that I don't think you know of, whom I've been acquainted with.

I'm waiting to hear of Olive's and then I am going to kill about five thousand Germans and celebrate. Perhaps thats rather strong but anyway thats what I'd feel like doing.

---

[6]"Nifley," as he calls it, is a German dish his Mother made. It consists of a combination of lumps of boiled noodles and fried onions and is more commonly referred to as "Spatzle." "Domies," another German dish, are a type of dumpling.

I have received several letters from home all together including one from Lewis, Alice, Laura and Frank.

This one as usual answers them all even though Alice did stick about half a dozen X X at the bottom of her letter and asked me to write her one individually.

Never mind! Yott[7] I'll write to you next time.

Have you received the check for $200? Please let me know as soon as possible.

I am getting the K.B. Press allright so if you care to continue sending it I will appreciate it. I don't think you will think or consider me vulgar to say that it comes in handy in many other cases besides just reading material.

Well, I must close hoping this finds you all well.

I am

As Ever,

Irving

---

[7]Irving's nickname for his sister, Alice.

Aviation Chief Machinist Mate Irving E. Sheely, back row center with bow tie, and other CPOs at Eastleigh Naval Air Station, England, November 1918 (Courtesy of Roger Sheely)

CHAPTER 7

Eastleigh and Home

September 18, 1918 to January 5, 1919

✧

[*During September and the first part of October, Lt. Kenneth MacLeish was at the U.S. Naval Aviation Assembly and Repair Base at Eastleigh in southern England. Eastleigh is just inland from the southcoast port of Southampton. He was busy overseeing the combat preparation of newly manufactured DH-4, 9, and 9A aircraft before they were ferried across the channel to Europe.*

Kenneth MacLeish had less than a month to live when his twenty-fourth birthday occurred on September 19, 1918. Irving was less than a year older when he became twenty-five on September 24, 1918. Yet in a September 18 letter, MacLeish says he has sent over to France for his old observer whom he refers to as "a good old horse," announcing that "he'll be a useful member of the flight department."

On September 24th, while serving in RAF 213 Squadron, Navy Lt. David Ingalls scored his fifth aerial victory and became the Navy's only World War I aerial ace. He was ordered to duty in England, and Lt. MacLeish was named as his replacement.

On September 26th, the largest American ground action of the war began in what was known as the Muese-Argonne offensive. It would culminate in the cessation of hostilities on November 11, 1918.

Lt. MacLeish reported for fighter plane duty with 213 Squadron on October 13, 1918. On the morning of October 14, MacLeish and others of the Squadron made a morning patrol flying Sopwith Camel fighters. They engaged a German flight, and MacLeish returned to base with his first aerial victory. MacLeish went out on a second patrol that afternoon and did not return.

Ten weeks and two days later, on December 26, 1918, a Belgian farmer, M. Rouse, who had been driven off his farm near Leffinghe by the German military, returned to reclaim his farm. Near his house, he found the body of Kenneth MacLeish.

Naval Aviator #74, Lt. Kenneth MacLeish was finally interred at Flanders Field American Cemetery and Memorial, Waregem, Belgium, in Plot B, Row 4, Grave 1. The white cross marker puts his date of death as October 15, 1918.

(Paine, The First Yale Unit, Vol. II, p. 360. Letter, American Battle Monuments Commission, Washington, D.C., May 21, 1980)]

Oct. 14, 1918

Dear Lewis,-

Suppose you will be suprised to hear that I am in England again. Well, I don't expect it to be for very long. However, I will have to be contented for the present as I have been sick and am still in the hospital. Guess I took a little cold during my two trips from [censored by cutout] to Dunkerque.[1]

While I was in Paris I sent another hundred dollars thru the YMCA. Glad you received the other check allright.

Tell Laura those pictures were fine. I am going to enclose a photo of myself. Hope you will like it. I have the negative and can send you more if you want them. I have had a couple of letters from my little French girl, but have not fully translated them yet.

My French is not growing very rapidly, however I jabber away with the Frenchmen as thou I know what I was talking about.

---

[1] The "cold" he speaks of may have been a case of the Spanish influenza epidemic that killed millions worldwide during 1918.

I have received all your letters but have not had the opportunity to answer them directly.

Well, I think I will close for this time hoping this finds you all well.

I am

As Ever,

Irving

{ *On November 1, 1918, while Irving was at Eastleigh, his grade was increased to that of "Chief Machinist Mate / Air," nineteen months after he had enlisted as Landsman for Machinist Mate Second Class. After the war the title would be revised to that of Aviation Chief Machinist Mate. (Irving E. Sheely, U.S. Navy Service Record from March 28, 1917 to August 22, 1922)*

The November 11, 1918 Armistice ended nineteen months of U.S. participation in European hostilities. During that period, the strength of U.S. Naval Aviation grew to a force of 6,716 officers and 30,693 men in Navy units and 282 officers, 2,180 men in Marine Corps units, with 2,107 aircraft, 15 dirigibles, and 215 kite and free balloons on hand. Of these numbers 18,000 officers and men and 570 aircraft had been sent abroad. ("United States Naval Aviation 1910–1970," p. 35; Van Wyen, "Naval Aviation in WWI," p. 89)

Within days after the Armistice went into effect, the Navy Assembly and Repair Base at Eastleigh, England, started shutdown procedures and, in less than a month, began embarking the men back to the states, leaving only a small guard force behind.

Each chapter of the 1919 book The Battle of Eastleigh *was written by a different veteran of service at that base. Eastleigh's Acting Chaplain, Lt. (j.g.) Norris L. Tibbetts U.S.N., wrote a poignant account in his chapter, "Homeward Bound," condensed and paraphrased here for brevity.*

On Monday, December 2, 1918, in mud and pouring rain, three drafts of men slogged out of the air base toward the train station in town where they boarded a train for Liverpool via London. There, they boarded the former German motorship Vaterland, captured by the Americans in 1917 and rechristened the USS Leviathan.

The first draft left at 6:30 p.m., the second draft at 8:45 p.m., and the third draft at 9:45 p.m. [Chief Petty Officer Irving E. Sheely, formerly of the U.S. Navy First Aeronautical Detachment, was in one of those drafts.] Despite the miserable cold and rain, the men sang "Hail, Hail the Gang's all Here" and "Long, Long Trail" as they marched to town. At the station, the Eastleigh Navy Band played, and the men boarded the trains with smiles almost too wide for the doors. Chaplain Tibbetts said that riding all night to Liverpool is not to be recommended but there was one "time out" for rolls, coffee, and chocolate served by the Red Cross at Leicester midway to Liverpool.

The 964-foot-long USS Leviathan looked inviting the next morning when they arrived at the only dock in England that could accommodate this, the largest of the world's transport vessels.

Hardships and deprivations for these World War I veterans were not yet over. The capacity of fresh water in the storage tanks of the Leviathan was sufficient to sustain only 4,500 passengers for about seven days, or the time required to sail from Hamburg to New York. This time they were boarding 11,300 men from all over the European theater, 1,500 of which were bedridden wounded.

In peacetime, it was possible to replenish the water completely at both the eastern and western ports, but at this eastern troop embarkation port, fresh water was exceedingly scarce. It was only possible to secure enough for feed-water for the boilers. Therefore, those veterans coming aboard had to endure with half the water for over twice as many people.

On Wednesday, December 4, 1918, the Leviathan sailed for Brest, France, landing there early Thursday. All hands were ordered to "turn to" *and load almost 7,500 tons of coal, enough for steaming eight days. This final European task was accomplished in three days.*

Chaplain Tibbetts said that when the men finished, they could have put on a minstrel show for the make-up was all there, and there was nothing with which to take it off.

Salt water with no soap was no match for coal dust. But the coal was at last aboard, and at 2:30 p.m. on Sunday, December 8, 1918, they steamed away from Brest, the next stop being NEW YORK, NEW YORK!!

It would indeed be a stretch of the imagination to call it a pleasant trip. No one can find much pleasure in life when the rough weather encountered during that cold, winter crossing caused the huge ship to pitch and roll constantly. Seasickness now added to the misery of that large number of dirty, thirsty, hungry, war-weary men.

Seven days later, the Statue of Liberty came into view, and for most of the men who went ashore that day, their final World War I ordeal was over.

For Irving, however, there was yet one more war-related duty to perform. Of all the letters he wrote between 1917 and 1918, none must have brought him more sadness and pain than when he shared his own sense of personal loss with the father of his battle-slain comrade and pilot, Lt. Kenneth MacLeish.}

Jan. 5, 1919

Mr. Andrew MacLeish
Glencoe, Ill.

My Dear Mr. MacLeish:

It was my pleasure to know Kenneth, your son, after coming into the Naval Flying Service. I met him in Dunkirk, France, in April, 1918, and had been with him up till his unfortunate flight across enemy lines. I will try and tell you something of our acquaintance, and what he afterward meant to me.

It was in the latter part of May when word came from Paris for all the chasse' pilots at Dunkirk to choose an observer, and proceed to Clermont-Ferrand and train at the Army Bombing School.

I will never forget the day when "Ken", as I always called him afterward, came to me and asked me to be his observer, and how delighted I was, for I considered it a great honor to fly with him. I had often admired his work in the air while on patrol over the North Sea.

Then he told me the intentions of the aviation forces, that we were to form a daylight squadron, and were the first of this kind to train at this school along with seventeen others.

We were sent there in June, and on completing our course in July, passing out with the highest marks in the class, we were sent to the front and carried out operations over the enemy lines from British Squadron 218 R.A.F.

Danger never entered our minds, and we successfully carried out bombing raids on Bruges and Zeebrugge, which were then of great military value.

Anti-aircraft guns were very active, and we were not left out when it was found out on landing at our aerodrome that shrapnel[2] had pierced our wings and tail.

During this time it was rumored about camp that some of the observers would have to fly with the Marine pilots. I remember what Ken said to us boys when we consulted him about this. This is what he told us, "Well, I guess not, Irv' isn't going to fly with any Marines."

How pleased I was to have him think and say so much of me.

I resolved to do everything in my power, if danger ever threatened him, to give my life if it ever should become necessary, to save his.

During these trips across the lines he taught me how to fly.

This was so I could save my own life if he were by chance hit by enemy shrapnel[2] or bullets.

It was the saddest moment in my life when word came to me in October, while I was ill, and in confinement in a hospital in England, that Ken had been shot down by the Huns.

I know you are proud of your boy, and the recollection of him who was the first to answer his county's call, and who insisted on the opportunity which led to his misfortune, will help you in this hour of sorrow.

Yours most sincerely,
Irving E. Sheely

(Kenneth MacLeish, Kenneth, A Collection of Letters, pp. 83–85)

[*Irving remained in Naval Aviation after the war. His first postwar duty station was NAS Anacostia, D.C., with a short, temporary assignment at Mitchell Field, Long Island. He was discharged on August 21, 1920, and immediately reenlisted for an additional two years. His next duty station was NAS Hampton Roads, Virginia. While at Hampton Roads the new Vought VE-7 training aircraft was introduced in numbers, and Irving and other Navy personnel did significant research on aircraft arresting gear for the Navy's forthcoming aircraft carrier then being converted from the USS Jupiter, one of the two colliers that transported the First Aeronautic Detachment to France in May 1917. During that period, Irving had a temporary tour of duty at Guantanamo Naval Base, Cuba, and was assigned to the USS Langley (CV-1), our first aircraft*

---

[2]These are the only two known instances of Irving spelling the word as: s-h-r-a-p-n-e-l instead of s-c-r-a-p-n-e-l. The whereabouts of the original letter is not known to this editor, and the spelling with an "h" is as it appeared in the 1919 book *Kenneth*. That editor probably recognized the error and corrected it.

carrier after it was commissioned on March 20, 1922. He accepted his final discharge from the U.S. Navy on August 22, 1922. (Irving E. Sheely, U.S. Navy Service Record from March 28, 1917 to August 22, 1922)

After his discharge, Irving married Dorothy Haskins from Preston Hollow, New York. They made their home along the Albany-Schenectady Road near Schenectady, New York, where they raised two sons, Lewis and Roger. During this period, Irving was a machine repairman for the B. T. Babbitt Company, makers of the household cleanser, "BAB-O," until his retirement in 1958.

Irving Edward Sheely, former U.S. Navy Aviation Chief Machinist Mate and World War I veteran, died December 16, 1962, at age sixty-nine. He, his wife Dorothy, and their son Lewis are buried in a small cemetery in the rural village of Potter Hollow, New York.]

APPENDIX A

Summary of Irving's Travels

1917 to 1918

Location	Arrived	Departed
299 Clinton Ave. Albany, N.Y.	—	Mar. 30, 1917
Pensacola U.S.N.A.S.	April 2, 1917	May 11,1917
Baltimore (USS Neptune)	May 14, 1917	May 23 1917
Norfolk Navy Base	May 24, 1917	May 25, 1917
St. Nazaire, France	June 9, 1917	June 10, 1917
Brest	June 10, 1917	June 13, 1917
Camaret	June 13, 1917	June 21, 1917
St. Raphael, Fr.N.A.S.	June 23, 1917	Aug. 28. 1917
Bordeaux	Aug. 29, 1917	Aug. 29, 1917
Moutchic U.S.N.A.S.	Aug. 29, 1917	Sept. 1, 1917
Cazeaux, Fr. N.A.S.	Sept. 2, 1917	Sept. 24, 1917
Moutchic U.S.N.A.S.	Sept. 24, 1917	Nov. 10, 1917
Paris	Nov. 11, 1917	Nov. 13, 1917
Dunkerque U.S.N.A.S.	Nov. 14, 1917	Nov. 23, 1917
Paris	Nov. 24, 1917	Nov. 28, 1917
London	Nov. 28, 1917	Nov. 30, 1917
Cranwell RNAS Base	Nov. 30, 1917	Dec. 13, 1917
Eastchurch RNAS Base	Dec. 13, 1917	Dec. 27, 1917
Leysdown RNAS Base	Dec. 27, 1917	Feb. 23, 1918

Location	Arrived	Departed
Paris	Mar. 2, 1918	??
Dunkerque U.S.N.A.S.	??	??
202 Squadron RAF★	Apr. 1, 1918	??
Dunkerque U.S.N.A.S.	May 6, 1918	??
Clermont-Ferrand, U.S. Army	June 5, 1918	??
Paris	July 3, 1918	??
Dunkerque U.S.N.A.S.	July 3, 1918	July 9, 1918
218 Squadron RAF★★	July 9, 1918	July 25, 1918
St. Ingleverte, N.B.G. Fld.A	Aug. 24, 1918	Oct. 1, 1918
HOSP. EASTLEIGH ENGLAND	Oct. 1, 1918	??
Armistice	Nov. 11, 1918	—
Sailed from Liverpool, Eng. Aboard USS *Leviathan*	Dec. 3, 1918	Dec. 4, 1918
Brest, France	Dec. 5, 1918	Dec. 8, 1918
New York City	Dec. 17, 1918	
299 Clinton Ave., Albany, N.Y.	Dec. 1918	End of Record

★Located at Bergues S.E. of Dunkerque, France
★★Located at Fretnum, S.W. of Calais, France

APPENDIX B

Training Notebook

MM2c(A) Irving E. Sheely U.S.N. 1917 to 1918

E'COLE DE TIR AERIEN
DE CAZAUX
FRANCE

E'COLE DE AVIATION
ST RAPHAEL
FRANCE

Irving E Sheely
US Aeronautic Sta
Pensacola Florida.

If lost Please return, and
liberal reward will be given.

Preparation for starting Motor

(1) Replenish gas tank through strainers

(2) See that sump has proper amount of oil

(3) Oil all exposed parts.

(4) See that propeller flange and bolts are tight and bolts are wired, propeller trued up within 1/8"

(5) See that radiator is filled

(6) See that magneto bolts, cylinder bolts and all other bolts are tight and properly cottered

(7) Check tappet clearance

(8) See that all wiring connections are tight

(9) See that all gas, oil and water pipes are in perfect condition

(10) Short both magnetos and test compression of cylinders by turning propeller.

Starting

(1) Short both magnetos. Open all gas cocks (It may be necessary to prime with gasoline through priming cocks, and to open compression relief cocks).

(2) Flood carburetor

(3) With throttle slightly open spin motor as rapidly as possible

(4) Retard spark, throw on ignition and with propeller or starting crank throw motor over compression

(5) As soon as started advance spark and adjust throttle to keep motor running slowly

Warming up

(1) With motor running slowly inspect oil and water circulation

(2) Short one magneto at a time to see that both are in working condition

(3) Gradually open up on throttle until full out

(4) Look carefully for any evidence of heating up

To stop motor

(1) Before stopping allow motor to run slowly for a minute or so then accelerate slightly, follow by shorting magnetos at the same time opening throttle (this to draw mixture into cylinders to prevent back firing and to facilitate restarting). If motor is through for day while still hot squirt kerosene into cylinders. 5 or 10 minutes after this, restart motor and run 3 or 4 minutes. This will facilitate restarting in the morning and will loosen up carbon deposits on pistons and stems.

Formula for determining PLAN

$$P = \text{Effective pressure}$$
$$L = \text{Length of stroke in feet}$$
$$A = \text{Piston area in sq inches}$$
$$N = \text{Revolution per minute}$$

$$\frac{P \times L \times A \times N \times \text{number of cylinders}}{33000 \times \text{\# of } \underset{(2)}{\times \text{per cycles}}} = H.P.$$

area of a piston is the square of the radius times 3.1416

For curtiss motor formula becomes

$$\frac{P L A N \times 8}{33000 \times 2} = H.P. \qquad \text{average pressure } 60 \text{ to } 80 \text{ #}$$

Material used in Curtiss Motor

Crank Shaft — Chrome Steel
Cam Shaft — Nickel Steel Contours C.H
Cam Shaft Followers   do
Wrist Pin   do
Connecting Rods — Steel Drop Forgy Mched
     "   " Bearing — Bronze lined white metal
     "   " Bolts   Nickel Steel
     "   " Siners Laminated Brass
Piston — Aluminum Alloy (Lynite)
     "   Rings Fine grade cast Iron
Cylinders   "   "   "   "
Water Jacket   Monel Metal
Crank Case — Aluminum casting
Oil Pump —   "   "
Cam Shaft Gear — Brass
Crank Shaft gears Mch Steel C.H
Magneto   "   "   "   "
Thrust Bearing Chrome steel
Rocker Arm — Cast   "
Intake yoke Alum Casting
Valve   Tungsten Steel

Valve springs — Spring steel
    "   "   Keepers Mch steel
Oil Pump Gears —   "   "
   "   "   Shaft —   "   "
   "   "   Gear Bracket — Brass casting
All Studs & Bolts Nickel Steel
Water Pump   Aluminum Casting
Impeller   Brass
Rocker arms connection's Brass
Push Rods Nikel Steel (Intake)
Pull "   Steel tubing (Exhaust)
Water outlet — Brass,

Valve Timeing

Curtiss	Hall Scott	Thomas + Sturtens
I.O. $\frac{1}{16}$ PTC	15°	10° BTC
I.C. $\frac{1}{2}$ P.B.C.	40°	45°
X.O. $\frac{13}{16}$ BBC	45°	45°
X.C. $\frac{1}{32}$ PBC*	10°	10°
Valve clearance .010 $\frac{1}{32}''$		.008 to .012
Magneto Breaks $\frac{7}{16}$ BTC. 27° (compression stroke)		25°

Firing order

12347856 — 153624		18547236
Bore $4\frac{1}{4}''$	5"	4"
Stroke 5"	7"	$5\frac{1}{2}''$

Cycle = An Object or a body moveing in one direction and performing one function in that move.

BTC = Before Top Center

PBC = Past Bottom center

BBC = Before Bottom center

P.T.C. Past Top Center.

---

* [I.O.—Intake Open; I.C.—Intake Closed; X.O./E.O.—Exhaust Open; X.C./E.C.—Exhaust Closed]

Oiling system of a Curtiss

OXX 2 or 3 – V type – 8 Cylinder – 4 Cycle Motor

(1) Forced feed to all bearings

(2) The oil is forced from the lowest point of the sump through a nickel plated copper tube to the rear end [of] the hollow cam shaft, past a pressure adjusting valve to all cam shaft bearings and timing gears then through ducts to the crank shaft bearings then through crank shaft, through to connecting rod bearings by centrifugal force to the walls of the piston drawn up by grooves to walls of cylinder thence through piston and oiling wrist pin. Returns to sump or reservoir to go over the same course again.

All valves and rocker arm pins are hand oiled. A removeable strainer is at the lowest point of the sump. Capacity of oil in reservoir in motor is four gal. Normal pressure by gauge is from 40 to 60 lbs. pressure per sq. in. by gauge.

Thomas & Sturtevant

Lubrication is of the complete forced circulating system.

The oil being supplied to the principal bearings under pressure by a rotary pump of the gear type which is operated by a gear from the crankshaft. The oil sump forms a reservoir from which it passes to a oil duct which connects the three crankshaft bearings.

From the rear end of this duct the oil passes through the base down to the rear crankshaft bearings and is distributed throughout its length to each of the camshaft bearings and is delivered to the water pump bearings directly above at which point the oil pressure gauge is located. From the rear crankshaft bearing, the oil enters the hollow crankshaft and passes through a hole in the crank arm to the big ends of the connecting rods of cylinders.

Material used in Curtiss Motor OXX [2]

Pistons—Aluminum Alloy
Piston Rings—Cast Iron
Piston Pins—Chrome Nickel Steel
Connecting Rods—Chrome Steel Forgings
Connecting (bearings)—Bronze backed, Babbit lined
Crankshaft—Chrome Nickel Steel
Crankshaft (bearings)— Bronze backed, Babbit lined
Crankcase—Aluminum Alloy Casting
Timing Gears—Manganese Bronze
Cylinders—Close Grained Cast Iron
Valves (Intake)—Nickel Steel
   (Exhaust)—Tungsten Steel
Valve Springs—Spring Steel
Rocker Arms—Drop Forged Steel
Cam Followers—Case Hardened Steel
Cam Shaft—Open Hearth Steel, Case Hardened
Magneto Gears—Steel
Water Pump—Aluminum housing
W.P. Impeller—Bronze
Water Piping—Steel Tubing, Nickel Plated
Exhaust Manifold—Welded Steel

Oiling System of the Hall Scott

The oil is pumped from the sump by a rotary pump through a lead up to a cooling chamber, thence through a lead back down to main duct situated in right side of crankcase. It is then delivered to the seven main bearings by seven oil leads from main duct. The crank journal and connecting rod bearings get their oil from the seepage from the . . . . [He stops at that point]

Hispano ~~Suiza~~
Suiza

		Clement Bayard
1	1	1 8
2	2	2 7
3	3	3 6
4	4	4 5

15374826 | 1 R 4 L 2 R 3 L 4 R

Valve clearance 2mm | 1 L 3 R 2 L

Firing Order of French motors

1400 R.P.M.

150 H.P.

8 cylinder

120 mm Alesage or Bore

130 mm Course or Stroke

Hispano Suiza Motor.

Cylinders are forged steel
screwed into casing or water.
Jacket which is all Aluminum.
Speed of Propeller is same as
crank shaft.

Hispano Suiza Valve Timing
Intake opens 10° 10' PTC 32 mm
"   closes 50°   PBC 165
Ex   Opens 45°   B.B.C. 150
Ex   closes 10° 10' PTC 32
    Magneto Breaks 64 mm B.T.C.
            20° 20'

Gas consumption 10.7 gal Per Hr

Oil " 3.2 lbs " "

Valve clearance 2 m/m

6/10	3 Key ways	31 m/m	6
7/10	1/2 turn 1 Key way	45 "	9
8/10	+ Key ways	50 "	2
9/10	1/2 turn 2 Keyways	56 "	5
	1 tooth 5 Keyways	62 "	8
1/0	3 Keyways less 1/2 turn	6 "	28
2/10	vertical shaft 1 K.W.	12 "	5
3/10	1/2 turn less 1 K.W.	18 "	8
4/10	2 Keyway	25 "	1
5/10	1/2 turn vertical shaft	31 "	4

Erecting of a Seaplane F.B.A
with a rotary motor

How to erect the centre section
5th and 6th Bulkhead

Operations must be made in the
order given

A To determine the difference of level
between the struts of the boat

1st Put the boat on flying level by
the means of a level placed between
the fifth and sixth bulkhead
starting from the fore part. This
level must be Zero in the two ways
longitudinal and transversal

The difference of level between a
and b must be between 50 and 54 m/m
and must have 110 to 120 m m incidence

If it is necessary make the difference
by lowering or raising the tail of the
boat. This new line obtained by
this way is definite and we must
conserve it till we finish the
assembling

(B) Build the holes into the plane
of the center section
Put the struts of the fore part
and aft part in their axis 22 m/m
from the transversal face of the
plane The forward struts are
shorter than the aft struts by
8 m/m   Length of forward struts
1 m 570 m m Length of aft
struts 1 m 578 m/m

(C) make the outline of the
centre section - Trace on
ground a line a b erect
perpendicular c d

Take width of overall of centre
section and note this width
as c-n at n erect ⊥ n R
Then take measure of gap
at forward strut as c.e.
and from point e erect ⊥ e.p.
Then c.e. = n.p.

Trace diagonals of rectangle
e.c.n.p. their point of intersect
is the crankshafts axis
for starting

Erect centre section on
this outline and strain
piano wires c.p. and e.n.
so as to make ▢ Rigid.
Place incidence wires and
properly strain them for that
a plumb line starting at the
after spar ought to pass
at a distance a from

forward spar. In Sevel a-b
we had between struts of boat

To find incidence of wing
place plumb line at trailing
edge + measure distance (b)
which is practical incidence E- to
erect lateral sections, assemble
wings on an outline, taking care
to put under struts some washers
for compensating thickness of
iron fittings that join sections.
keep incidence equal to that
of centre section.
If motor turns anti clockwise
(facing the propeller and engine) increase
incidence of right sections say
15 m/m for compensating
overturning of motor torque.
F= To regulate ailerons
Lateral section being erected
on boat, assemble the

"differencial or wire of conjugation" so that two ailerons fall or sink down their thickness and about 1 cm more. Then put stick handle in a verticle position and adjust wires to ailerons and let sufficient slack.

To erect fittings of tail plane (fixed) put axis of rudder tube in a verticle position. Adjust stabilizer to the fixed plane on the ground before erecting. Put plane on its axis and adjust incidence (according to the number of and position of passengers) which varies from 20 to 100 m/m Regulate it definately after first flight. If machine attempts to dive down decrease incidence and vice versa for diving up.

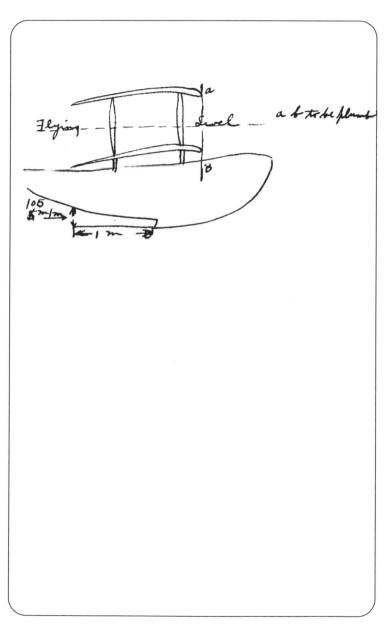

HISPANO SUIZA

DIAMETER OF DISC 360 m/m

Admission   Intake
Compression   Compression
Detente   Firing
Eshappent   Exhaust

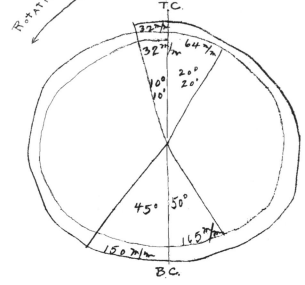

Hispano Suiza

1 - assembling   Magneto breaker
2 - Regulation   points 4/10 m/m
3 - Inspection   Spark Plug
4 - Dismounting   Points 4/10 m/m
Four cycles
Eight Cylinders
Vee Type
Bore 120 m m
Stroke 130 m m
H.P. 150
Speed 1400 R.P.M.
Double Ignition
Firing order 1243 Left
           4312 Right
This is read from the
timing gears
Gas Consumption 4 8 Liters Put
               (10 gal)
Oil   "   1 Kilo 300 grams .
               (5 $\frac{2}{3}$ lbs)
Weight complete
     150 Kilos   (387 $\frac{1}{2}$ lbs)

Diss Assembling of Parts

I   Take off the carburetor
     and heating Jacket
II   Take off intake manifold
III Take off breather pipe
IV   "   " Tachmeter
V   "   " Seads of magnetos
     "   out Plugs sparks
     "   off Air Pump
VI   "   "   Water "}
              Oil   "}
         which are coupled together
VII "   off Magnetos
     Disconnect magneto gear
     driving Jacket.
     Take off bolts of magneto
     Lift magneto heigh enough
     to get out dowel pins and
     then magneto will come off
     Dismount starting crank and
     mechanisms.

Remove cam shaft, oil pipes and then cylinder blocks. Take care not to let pistons fall. Remove all valves and don't get them mixed up.

Remove sump and take out crank shaft and take care not to let lower half of bearings fall.

Inspect all repaired parts. Carburetor, try jets, float, and throttle. See that manifolds are not cracked.

Inspect leads from magneto.

Test air pump and replace packing if necessary.

Inspect water pump and replace stuffing box

Clean oil pump and test springs and see that they are in good condition.

Test all bearings and see that
all are properly adjusted.
Clean lubricating system
thoroughly. Scrape all carbon
and clean with gasoline.
  Clean all parts with gasoline
before mounting and oil
bearings and friction
surfaces with castor oil.

Renault aviation motor
H Power 220
Cylinders 12
Magnetos 2
Bore   125 m/m
Stroke   150 m/m
R.P.M.   1200
I.O.   5°.50'   0.6 m/m P.J.C.
I.C.   44°   10.5 m/m O.B.C.
E.O.   48°.30'   20 m/m B.B.C.
E.C   18°50'   05. m/m P.J.C.
  magneto Breaks 28° B.J.C.

Clement Bayard
H Power 150   8 cyl 2 in Block
R.P.M. 1400
Bore   120 m/m
Stroke 140
Firing Order 15374826
gas consumption 50 liters per Hour
Oil   "   3   "   "   "

I.O. Top center a little before but never after allowed

I.C. 14 to 16 m/m P.B.C.

E.O. 19 to 21 " B.B.C.

E.C. Top centre. #a-9

Salmson Aviation motor

Bore 125 m m

Stroke 140 m m

F.O. 1 3 5 7 9 2 4 6 8 (all right 1 to 16)

Mag Breaks 15 m/m B.J.C.

1500 R.P.M. gas con / 50 liters per hour
             Oil "   2   "   " "

Clerget Aviation motor

Rotary type

magnetos 2

Bore 120 m/m

Stroke 140 "

R.P.M. 1250

I.O. top centre

I C 52° P.B.C

E.O. 64° BBC

E.C. Top centre

Mag Breaks 26° B.J.C.

H Power 110

Loiraine aviation motor
H Power   160
Cylinder   8
Type   Vee
Bore   120 m/m
Stroke   140 "
Fires   1 5 3 7 4 8 2 6
I.O.   45°   124 m/m.3 P BC
I.O.   5°   0   "   PTC*
E O   50°   120 m/m.8 BBC
E.C.   13°   2   " 3   PTC
May Breaks 32° 13 m/m.6 B.T.C.

Canton Unne aviation motor
I.O. Top centre
I.C. 45° 16 m/m PBC
E.O. 55° 22 m/m.5 B.B.C.
E.C. Top centre
Fires   35° B.T.C.

---

*[Irving began this entry with Intake Closed data instead of Intake Open. He probably meant to write I.O. 5° 0 m/m PTC *before* I.C. 45° 124 m/m .3 PBC.]

Vickers Machine Gun

1st Phase

Recoil of the whole mobile parts to the verticle position of the cocking handle.

1– The gas acting on the shell case a fraction, later by the gas on the muzzel cup

Lock

1– Unlocking
2– Opening of the breach
3– Extraction
4– Drawing back of the firing pin and cocking of the Sear

Feeding

1– Extraction of live cartridge from the belt
2– Feed palls move to the right

2nd Phase

Forward movement of barrel going to firing position
1– Action of the fore arm on the roller by force of inertia

Lock

1– Extractor forced down
2– Preparation for ejection

Feeding

1– Fall of the extractor
2– Preparation for the introduction of a live cartridge into the barrel

3- Feeding palls move to the left

4- Maximum extension of fusse spg.

3rd Phase

Return of the breach to its firing position

Action

1- Action of fusse spring

Lock

1- Extractor in upward movement

2- Ejection

3- Locking of breach

4- Sear and trigger release

5- Firing

Feeding

1- Introduction of live cartridge

2- Upward movement of extractor

3- Gripping of cartridge

-Fini-

Vickers Machine Gun

Recoil of Barrel and Breach

1- Backward movement of whole mobile part

2- Breaking of the straight line by action of the roller on tail of the crank

3- Extraction of empty shell also new one from belt

4– Cocking of trigger
5– Cocking of Sear

Barrel goes forward

1– Extractor falls and allows live cartridge to get in place
2– Extractor falls and prepares the ejection

Action of fusse spring

1– Introduction of live cartridge into barrel
2– Extractor goes up by action of side levers and ext. levers on breach
3– New cartridge seized by extractor

(2) Extraction of empty cartridge

[Am not sure what is going on with his number sequence at this point as he turns a page in his notebook]

3– Breach locked by straight line of connecting line
4– Sear is released
5– Firing of cartridge by action of thumb on trigger bar and trigger.

Action of gun backward

Fusse spring should have 6 to 8 lbs. tension
1– All the way down = Lack of precussion, broken firing pin or bad cartridge
2– Spring too weak or rim of cartridge too thick
3– Bad presentation of cartridge
4– Shell case too thick
5– Shell case broken

6– Gib spring broken allowing cartridge to fall

7– Spring too strong or not enough gas (Shutter closed)

8– Fusse spring broken

Correction of Target

Target Deflection = $\dfrac{Vb \times D}{Wm}$

Correction of Shooter

Shooter Deflection = $\dfrac{Vt \times D}{Vo}$

Vb   = Velocity of Target

D   = Distance from Target

Wm = Average speed of bullet – 680mps

Vt   = Velocity of Shooter

Vo   = Initial speed of bullet – 740mps

Q is point to aim at

P is point where bullet will hit aeroplane

When sights are in line of fuzelage the angle is at 0 degrees

Lewis Machine Gun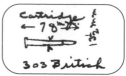

2500 Klo per sq. cm. for tracer ⎫
3000 Klo per sq. cm. for tracer ⎭   on bullet

Always have the large hole of the gas escapement for aviation shooting.

Weights – 29 lbs.

Has – 62 parts

Spring Tension – 18 to 20 lbs.

Magazine holds 47 cartridges (small) mag caliber 303

1/100 part of the gas is used to operate the mechanism, on the head of the piston

Action of backward movement

1– Firing pin goes back
2– Unlocking   1/8 of a turn
3– Extraction
4– Ejection
5– Cocking

Action of forward movement

1– Release of Sear
2– Cartridge put in chamber
3– Extractor grips rim of cartridge
4– Locking of Breach
5– Firing

Feeding backward movement

1– Feeding plate moves to the left
2– Action of feed jaw moving the magazine to the left
3– Presentation of cartridge and resting on the feeding ridges

[Notebook is all done in pencil and next two lines have been erased. Another sequence is then begun.]

1– Feeding plate moves to the right
2– Locking of magazine by palls
3– Cartridge fed into the ridges by the guide spring.

Shooters Deflection

Klm. per Hr.

	50	80	100	110	120	130	140	150	160	170	180	190	200	210	250	m.p. sec.
100	2.	3	3.5	4.	4.5	5.	5.5	6	6.5	7	7.5	8.5	9.5			69 40
200	3.	6.	7.5	8.5	10	10.5	11.5	12	13	13.5	14.5	16.	16.5	19		61 10
300	5.	9.	11.	12.5	13.5	14.5	16.	17.	18	19	20.5	21.5	22.5	25	28	55 60
400	7.	12.	15	16.5	18	19.5	21	22.5	24	25.6	27	29	30	33	3.7	52 80
500	9.5	15	19	20.6	22.5	24.5	26	28	30	32	34	36	37	41	47	50 00
600	11	18	22.5	25	27	29	32	34	36	38	41	43	45	60	5C	47 25
700	13	21	26	29	32	34	37	39	42	45	47	50	52	68	6C	44 50
1000	19	30	38	41	45	49	53	56	60	64	68	71	76	85	94	41 70
																39 00
																36 10
																33 40
																30 60
																27 80
																22 20
																13 90

1 Klm = 5/8 of a mile.

Distance of Combat in Meters

Target Deflection

Klm. per Hr. 250 18 36 54 72 90 100 110 120 130 140 150 160 170 180 190 200 220

Distance of Combat in Meters																			m. p. sec.
100′	9.5	0.7	1.5	2.	3.	4.	4.5	4.5	5.	5.5	6.	6.5	7	7.5	8.	8.5			61 10
200′	21.	1.6	3.	4.	4.5	6.	6.5	8	10	11	11.5	12.5	13.6	14.	15.	16.	16.5	18.5	55 60
300′	33.	2.5	4.5	6.6	7.	9.5	10.5	13.	14.5	15.5	17	18.6	19.5	21.	22.	23.5	25	26. 29	52 80
400′	46.	3.5	6.5	7.	10.	13.	14.5	18.5	20.	22.	24.	25.5	27.	29.	31.	33.	35.	37. 40.	50 00
500′	59.	4.	8.5	12.	13.	17	19	21.5	26	28	31.	33	35	37	40	42	45	47 52	47 25
600′	75.	6.5	11.	15.	16.	21.5	24	27.5	29	32.5	33	39	42	45	48	51	54	57 60 66	44 50
700′	90	6.5	13.	18	19.6	26.	29	36	40	43	47	51	54	58	61	65	69	72 79	41 70
																			39 00
																			36 10
																			33 40
																			30 60
																			27 80
																			22 20
																			20 00
																			15 00
																			13 90
																			10 00
																			5 00
																			69 40

Outer Circle   Aero diving   Angle 90°
middle "   "   level   Angle 90°
            Or "   diving   Angle 45°
Inner "   Aero climbing Angle 90°
    or "   level   Angle 45°
    or "   diving   Angle 30°
Inside the Inner circle = Aero climbing 45°
                        Aero level   30°
Further Inside aero climbing   30°
All this used with the average speed
of a 150 Klm per hr.
The axis of flight must always be
directly through the centre.

Cazaux Deflector.

For example
$VT. = 160$ K.m.h.

$D = 200$ m

$l = .60$ m

Find g

By table

$g' = 60$ m/m for 1m

I have .60 of 1m

g will $= \dfrac{60}{.60}$

$\dfrac{}{36.00}$

$g = 36$ m/m

$$\frac{l}{g} = \frac{D}{S}$$

to find

$$g = \frac{l \times S}{D}$$

Simple proportion

Cartridges

Lewis	– 303
French	– 7.65 mm
Length overall	– 78.0 mm
Length of bullet	– 32.5 mm
Diameter of rim	– 13.4 mm
Projection of rim	– 0.75 to 0.85 mm
Thickness of rim	– 1.5 mm
Weight of bullet	– 25.0 grammes
Gas Pressure	– 2700 Klo per sq. cm.
Temperature	– 3000° centigrade
Diameter of case	– 11.7 mm (close to rim)

APX Lewis perforating bullet

Color	– Dark Brown
Jacket	– 90% Copper, 10% Zinc
Centre	– Tempered Steel
Powder	– BN3F French 2.30 grammes
Weight of bullet	– 9.50 grammes

S.P.G. Tracer

chilled lead and aluminum alloy

Powder	– Cordite 250 grammes
Weight of bullet	– 10.70 grammes

Colt Cartridges

Aluminum and lead center
Nickel and copper case

Powder	– 2.50 grammes
Weight of bullet	– 11.20

Initial speed	– 740 meters per second
at 300m	– 645 " " "
at 500m	– 580 " " "
at 300m	–
at 500m	–

27 c m →
1 m   VCO 7.80

Burkingham Incendary Bullet

Color	– Aluminum
Inside of	White phosphor and lead
Weight	– 8.70
VCO	– 785

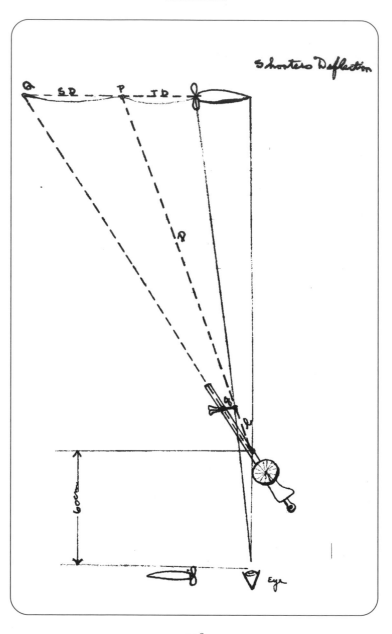

Correcteur
Reille Soult

Target Deflection

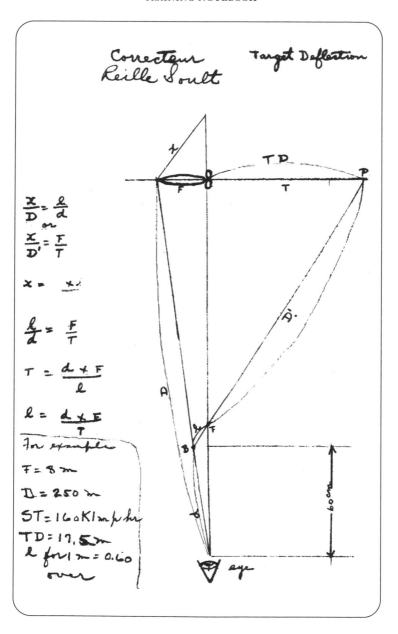

$$\frac{x}{D} = \frac{\ell}{d}$$

or

$$\frac{x}{D'} = \frac{F}{T}$$

$$x = \frac{x \cdot}{}$$

$$\frac{\ell}{d} = \frac{F}{T}$$

$$T = \frac{d \times F}{\ell}$$

$$\ell = \frac{d \times F}{T}$$

For example

$F = 8\,m$

$D = 250\,m$

$ST = 160\,Klm\,p\,hr$

$TD = 17.5\,m$

ℓ for $1\,m = 0.60$

over

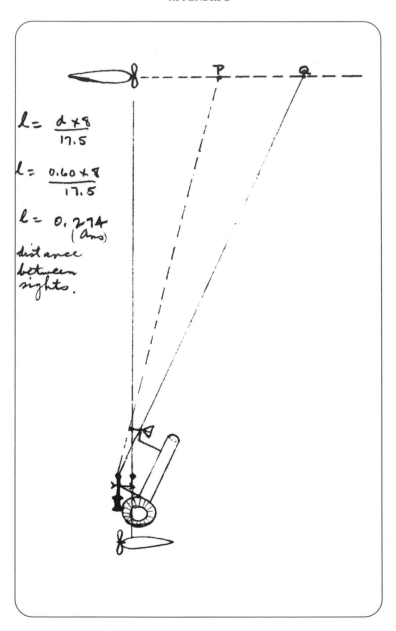

$$l = \frac{d \times 8}{17.5}$$

$$l = \frac{0.60 \times 8}{17.5}$$

$$l = 0.274$$
(Ans)

distance
between
sights.

To find point Q. Aim through
two fix sights
To find point P. Aim through
one fix sight and one mobile sight

Correct deviations for
shooting from a U D of 9 0 Knots
at a machine of 100 Knots
From rear sight to front sight. 22.8 cm
From Eye to rear sight. 60 cm
Wind var   8.3 m/m .

From rear sight to front sight 69 cm
From Eye to rear sight 50 cm
Wind Var   6.9 m/m

ʃ

[What follows was found in the final pages of the notebook. It was written in ink.]

Zenith Carburator
Zenith Principals

It is a nozel compound type. One jet counteracts the faults of the other jet giving a proper mixture at all times.

A carburator is a mechanical device used on gasoline motors which functions are to mix and control gas and air before entering the cylinders.

The functions are to mix gas and air properly for proper combustion at proper intervals.

C & H compound

$C_6 H_{14}$
$C_n H_{2n+12}$ = gasoline [Correct formula for gasoline: $C_n H_{2n+2}$]

180 cu.ft. of air to 1 lb gas gives proper combustion
19.45 parts of air to 1 part of gas gives proper mixture

Instruments used in aeroplanes

Compass
Altimeter
Air speed meter or pitot tube
Inclinometer
Drift meter
Tachometer
Oil Gauge   Gas pressure gauge (feed system)
Oil Pressure Gauge   Motor meter
Gasoline Gauge   Sextant
Angle of Attack   Clock

Bibliography

✧

Unpublished Documents

American Battle Monuments Commission. Letters to L. Sheely.

Lasher, Ens. Herbert. Diary entry for May 6, 1918.

————. Letters to L. Sheely.

Log of RAF 202 Squadron using DH-4 aircraft for reconnaissance patrols. Public Record Office, Kew, England.

Log of RAF 218 Squadron using DH-9 aircraft as bombers. Public Record Office, Kew, England.

Log of USS *Jupiter* (AC-3) 1917. National Archives, Washington, D.C.

Log of USS *Neptune* (AC-8) 1917. National Archives, Washington, D.C.

Log of U.S. NAS Dunkerque, France, spring 1918. National Archives, Washington, D.C.

Log of The USNA Northern Bombing Group. National Archives, Washington, D.C.

Sheely, Irving E. Diary kept from March 28, 1917 to February 8, 1918.

————. Letters written to family and friends, 1917–1918.

————. Training Notebook created while in school at French N.A.S. St. Raphael, July 1917.

————. U.S. Navy Service Record from March 28, 1917 to August 22, 1922.

Taylor, Stewart K., renowned Canadian/British military historian. Letters of historical data.

Whiting, Cdr. Kenneth, USN. "History of the 1st Aeronautic Detachment, USN." November 29, 1918. National Archives, Washington, D.C.

Periodicals

Almanac, Information Please, 1989. Boston: Houghton Mifflin, 1989.

Albany *Times Union* (newspaper). March 29, 1917 (probable date).

Huff, R. J. *Wings and Things of the World*, No. 13 (Fall 1990).

Miller, Thomas G., Jr., ed. "Naval Aviation Overseas, 1917–1918." *Cross & Cockade Journal* (Society of WWI Aero Historians) 4, No. 1 (1963): 52–83.

Morris, Chris. "The History of Royal Navy Flying Badges." *Wings and Things of the World*, No. 13 (Fall 1990): 36.

Sheely, L. D. "Irving Edward Sheely—Naval Observer." *Over The Front Journal* (League of WWI Aviation Historians) 3, No. 2 (1988): 99–133.

Shirley, Noel. "John Lansing Callan—Naval Aviation Pioneer." *Over The Front Journal* (League of WWI Aviation Historians) 2, No. 2 (1987): 180–85.

Skelton, Marvin L. "Recollections of 1st. Lt. Karl C. Payne, No. 20 Aero Squadron, U.S.A.S." *Cross & Cockade Journal* (Society of WWI Aero Historians) 21, No. 4 (1980): 307–10.

Sprague, G. E. "Flying Gobs." *Liberty Magazine*, Jan. 7, 14, 21, 1939.

"United States Naval Aviation, 1910–1970." *Navair* 00-80P-1. Washington, D.C.: U.S. Government Printing Office, 1970.

Van Wyen, Adrian O. "Naval Aviation in WWI." *Naval Aviation News*. Washington, D.C.: Chief of Naval Operations, U.S. Government Printing Office, 1969.

Books

Bolle, Frederick N. *The Battle of Eastleigh*. U.S.N.A.F., 1919.

Chalif, D. *Military Pilot and Aircrew Badges of the World, 1870 to Present*. Vol. I, *Europe (Albania-Hungary)*. San Jose, Calif.: Roger J. Bender Publishing Co., 1982.

Clark, Donald. *Wild Blue Yonder.* Seattle, Wash.: Superior Publication Co., 1972. [Collection of S. K. Taylor.]

Hinding, Andrea. *Proud Heritage: A History in Pictures of the YMCA in the United States.* Virginia Beach: Donning Co., 1988.

Hopkins, C. H. *History of the Y.M.C.A. in North America.* New York: Association Press, 1951.

Jones, H. A. *War in the Air.* Vol. IV. London: Oxford University Press, 1934. [Collection of S. K. Taylor.]

Lamberton, W. M., comp. *Reconnaissance and Bomber Aircraft of the 1914–1918 War.* Edited by E. F. Cheesman. Letchworth, England: Harleyford Publ., 1962.

———, comp. *Fighter Aircraft of the 1914–1918 War.* Edited by E. F. Cheesman. Letchworth, England: Harleyford Publ., 1960.

MacLeish, Kenneth. *Kenneth: A Collection of Letters written by Lieut. Kenneth MacLeish, U.S.N.R.F.C.* Edited by Martha [Mrs. Andrew] MacLeish. Chicago: privately printed, 1919.

Moseley, George Clark. *Extracts from the Letters of George Clark Moseley, During the Period of the Great War.* Privately printed, 1923.

Munson, Kenneth. *Bombers, Patrol and Reconnaissance Aircraft 1914–1919.* London: Blandford/MacMillan/Cassell PLC, 1968.

Nowarra, Heinz J. *Marine Aircraft of the 1914–1918 War.* Letchworth, England: Harleyford Publ., 1966.

Paine, Ralph D. *The First Yale Unit.* Vols. I–II. New York: Riverside Press, 1925.

Roscoe, Theodore. *On the Seas and in the Skies.* New York: Hawthorne Books, 1970.

Savage-Lewis Automatic Machine Gun, Air-Cooled, Gas-Operated, Model 1915. Utica, N.Y.: Savage Arms Co. Reprint, Forest Grove, Oregon: Normount Armament Co., 1970.

Smith, Herschel. *Aircraft Piston Engines.* New York: McGraw-Hill, 1981.

Stock, James W. *Zeebrugge—23 April 1918.* Battle Book #31. New York: Ballantine Books, Random House, 1974.

Swanborough, Gordon, and Peter Bowers. *United States Navy Aircraft since 1911*. New York: Putnam, 1968.

Thetford, O. G., comp. *Aircraft of the 1914–1918 War*. Edited by D. A. Russell. Letchworth, England: Harleyford Publ., 1954.

van Deurs, Rear Adm. George, U.S.N. (Ret.) *Wings for the Fleet*. Annapolis: Naval Institute, 1966.

Index

Lawrence D. Sheely has been researching the World War I U.S. Naval Aviation experiences of his uncle, Irving E. Sheely, since Irving's death in late 1962. His research was aided by membership in The Aviation Historical Society of Central New York, League of World War I Aviation Historians, The Society of World War I Aero Historians, The First World War Aviation Historical Society, and The American Aviation Historical Society.

During forty years with the General Electric Company Sheely progressed from an Apprentice to a Mechanical Design Engineer. Several times throughout that career, he was cited for inventions and published articles related to the military electronic equipment produced by his department. In 1986 he retired to Florida and wrote about his own World War II flying experiences and technical articles about motor homes. In between, he continued research on the history of U.S. Naval Aviation and the preparation of this book.